Christ
in the
Tabernacle

Christ in the Tabernacle

A.B. SIMPSON

Christian Publications
Camp Hill, Pennsylvania

Christian Publications
3825 Hartzdale Drive, Camp Hill, PA 17011

Faithful, biblical publishing—since 1883

ISBN: 0-87509-361-2
LOC Catalog Card Number: 85-70720
© 1985 by Christian Publications
All rights reserved
Printed in the United States of America

94 95 96 97 98   12   11   10   9   8

Unless otherwise indicated, Scripture taken from the
HOLY BIBLE,
AUTHORIZED KING JAMES VERSION.

The cover photo by Steve Miller shows the table of
showbread at the Hebrew Tabernacle, Reproduction,
Mennnonite Information Center, Lancaster, PA 17602.

Cover Design by
Robert A. Baddorf

CONTENTS

The Tabernacle a Type of Christ

A ND THE LORD *spake unto Moses, saying, speak unto the children of Israel, that they bring me an offering: of every man that giveth it willingly with his heart ye shall take my offering. And this is the offering which ye shall take of them; gold, and silver, and brass, and blue, and purple, and scarlet, and fine linen, and goats' hair, and rams' skins dyed red, and badgers' skins, and shittim wood, oil for the light, spices for anointing oil, and for sweet incense, onyx stones, and stones to be set in the ephod, and in the breastplate.*

And let them make me a sanctuary; that I may dwell among them. According to all that I shew thee, after the pattern of the tabernacle, and the pattern of all the instruments thereof, even so shall ye make it.

And they shall make an ark of shittim wood: two cubits and a half shall be the length thereof, and a cubit and a half the breadth thereof, and a cubit and a half the height thereof. Exodus 25:1-10

The Tabernacle is the greatest of all the Old Testament types of Christ. It was all one great object lesson of spiritual truth. In its wonderful furniture, its priesthood and its worship we see with a vividness that we find nowhere else the glory and grace of Jesus and the privileges of His redeemed people.

Just as in the architect's plan we can understand the future building better, so in this pattern from the mount we can understand as nowhere else that glorious temple of which Christ is the cornerstone. And we also, as living stones, are built up in Him "a spiritual house, an holy priesthood, to offer up spiritual sacrifices, acceptable to God by Jesus Christ" (1 Peter 2:5).

The Form and Structure of the Tabernacle

The Tabernacle was an oblong structure about 45 feet long and 15 feet wide and high. It was constructed of boards of shittim wood, a peculiarly indestructible material, overlaid with gold and fastened in sockets with tenons of silver and brass. It was covered with three tiers of skins and a fine interior lining of costly curtains. These curtains were adorned with embroidered symbolic figures of the highest beauty and spiritual significance.

The external covering of the roof was of rough badgers' skins to protect the Tabernacle from inclement weather. The exact form of the roof is a matter of dispute, some believing it to have been pitched at an angle and some an arched or a flat surface.

The Tabernacle itself was divided into two chambers of unequal size by a magnificent curtain called a veil. The larger division was 15 by 30 feet. It was called the Holy Place, open to the ministering priest only—not to the common people. The Holy Place was protected from the outer court by a curtain door, also of blue, purple and scarlet, past which none but cleansed and consecrated priests might go.

Its articles of furniture were three. There was the golden candlestick, which was its only light, there being no windows. There was the table of show-bread—12 loaves fresh-baked for each Sabbath, crowned with pure frankincense, that remained displayed for one week and then were eaten by the priests. And there was the golden altar of incense, with its accompanying censer, where pure frankincense was continually offered. From that altar once a year on the great Day of Atonement the high priest with the golden censer took burning coals and smoking incense in his hands, passed through the mysterious veil, entered alone the Holy of Holies and there made atonement for the people in the immediate presence of God.

The inner Holy of Holies was a perfect cube, 15 feet square. It contained the ark of the covenant, over which was the mercy seat. The mercy seat was the ark's top, and it consisted of a solid plate of gold. Springing from this and formed of the same piece of gold, hovered the cherubim, symbolic figures representing the faces of the four typical forms of the animate creation—man, ox, eagle and lion.

Between the meeting wings of the cherubic figures shone the Shekinah or visible divine glory, a luminous cloud of transcendent brightness that perhaps arose and expanded into the pillar of cloud and fire that hovered above the Tabernacle, leading the march of Israel. This Holy of Holies was God's special presence chamber and throne of grace and glory. None ever entered it except the high priest, and he only once a year.

Surrounding the Tabernacle was a court, an enclosure 87 by 175 feet, with an opening or gate on the eastern side. Into this court all the people might come.

Two objects of ceremonial worship stood in the court. Near the gate was the brazen altar of burnt offering. There the sacrifices of burnt offering were presented, the blood sprinkled and the fire kept ever burning, from which the altar of incense was supplied. All parts of the Tabernacle had to be sprinkled with blood from that altar. It was the only way of access to the presence of God.

Farther in was the brazen laver, a vast basin made from the metal mirrors of the women of Israel. Perhaps the exterior was polished, forming thus a mirror as well as a fountain. If so, it would have enabled the priests at once to see their uncleanness in the metal and then to wash it away in the water it contained. The laver was for the purification of the priests as they entered the sanctuary, and no one could pass through the door until he had washed in that fountain.

The gate to the outer enclosure was always open. It had no hangings as did the two inner doorways. All might freely go into the Lord's courts and bring their offerings for sin and uncleanness.

Outside the outer gate was the camp of Israel. It formed a vast square around the Tabernacle.

Three tribes were on each side. The tribe of Judah was on the east, opposite the Tabernacle entrance. Out beyond the camping tribes of Israel there continually burned the fire without the camp, where the bodies of the sin offerings were consumed and the refuse of the camp burned.

Such was this simple and wonderful structure—God's first sanctuary and the type of all that is sacred and precious in the person and work of Christ and the privileges of our heavenly calling.

The Erection of the Tabernacle and Its Subsequent History

There are two accounts in Exodus of the construction of the Tabernacle. First, in Exodus 25:40 we have the Tabernacle as it was planned in heaven and shown to Moses on the mount as a pattern. It is the type of Christ set forth from eternity in the counsels of divine love. This is a type of our Redeemer, prepared for us from before the foundation of the world and revealed in successive types and prophecies long before His actual enfleshment and life on earth. Moses built the Tabernacle according to an actual model that God had shown him during the 40 days he spent on Mount Sinai. So Christ was born, lived and died exactly as previous revelation prophesied.

In Exodus 32 and 33 the dark interval of sorrow and rebellion is described, during which the people transgressed the covenant they had just entered into, showing most painfully their need of the salvation God had been preparing for them.

It typifies man's fall and his failure under the

old dispensation. Christ had been already provided, but man must feel the need of divine salvation by the actual experience of sin. It is touching beyond degree to know that all the time man was rebelling against his God, God's remedy was waiting in that mount of grace.

Then in Exodus 34 we come to the second stage in the history of the Tabernacle—its actual erection according to the divine plan already shown. It was made possible through the freewill offerings of the people and the skill and workmanship of the men whom God had specially endued for this purpose. Two men were particularly called and qualified by the gifts of the Holy Spirit in sacred art to originate and execute all the Tabernacle's symbolic decorations. The women of Israel were similarly prepared and enabled to make ready its costly materials. So its entire erection was through the supernatural gifts of the Holy Spirit as well as the divine plan that was revealed to Moses.

During the 40 years of Israel's wilderness life, the Tabernacle was borne from place to place by the faithful Levites who had been appointed for this special ministry. After Israel's entrance into Canaan, the Tabernacle remained for a time at Gilgal and afterwards was established at Shiloh, which became the religious center of national worship.

During the period of the Judges we lose sight of the Tabernacle for a season as Israel is subjugated and humiliated. But we find it afterward in Nob, in the neighborhood of Jerusalem, in the reign of David. And finally it was established on Mount Zion through the piety of this good king, where it remained until superseded by the more magnificent Temple of Solomon.

Solomon's Temple, however, was only a more splendid edition of the same building, containing all the essential features of the Tabernacle. The Temple added a higher degree of splendor and so typified the future glories as the Tabernacle typified the grace of Christ and His redemption.

A Representation of Christ

The Tabernacle was designed to represent and prefigure the most important teachings of the Scriptures with reference to Christ, to the Church, to the individual Christian.

As a type of Christ, the very word *Tabernacle* is used with reference to Him in the opening chapter of the Gospel of John. "The Word was made flesh, and dwelt [tabernacled] among us, (and we beheld his glory, the glory as of the only begotten of the Father,) full of grace and truth" (1:14).

Again, in Hebrews 9 the writer, after describing the structure of the ancient sanctuary, applies it all to the person and work of Christ.

The points of comparison are almost limitless. Among them these may be mentioned:

(1) The positioning of the Tabernacle, which was entered from the camp of Judah, suggests that Christ was born of the tribe of Judah.

(2) The indestructible wood and pure gold suggests Christ's perfect humanity on the one hand and His supreme divinity on the other.

(3) The colors that were so constantly mingled in

the Tabernacle, especially the prevailing hues of white, blue, scarlet and purple, all point to qualities in Jesus: the white, His spotless purity; the blue, His heavenly origin; the scarlet, His sufferings and death; the purple, His kingly glory.

(4) The external plainness of the Tabernacle in contrast with the internal glory—the badgers' skins without and the gold and Shekinah glory within— proclaim the lowliness of Christ's earthly state and the beauty and glory of His character and inner presence as He reveals Himself to the soul that abides in Him.

(5) The contrast between the Tabernacle and the Temple, the one a shifting tent exposed to constant vicissitude and humiliation, the other combining in itself all the glory of earth and heaven, suggests to us the earthly life of our Lord and His exaltation and the kingly glory of His millennial reign.

(6) The Tabernacle was God's meeting place with Israel. "There I will meet with thee . . . from between the two cherubims" were His own words (Exodus 25:22). "When Moses was gone into the tabernacle of the congregation to speak with him, then he heard the voice of one speaking unto him . . . from between the two cherubims" (Numbers 7:89). And so the Lord Jesus Christ is the only way of access to the Father and fellowship with heaven. "If a man love me, he will keep my words: and my father will love him, and we will come unto him, and make our abode with him" (John 14:23).

(7) The Tabernacle was the place of sacrifice. Its most vivid spectacle was the flowing and the sprinkled blood. Every part of the Tabernacle

speaks to us of the sacrifice of Christ.

(8) Not only was the Tabernacle the place of sacrifice, but it was also the place of cleansing. The blood atoned for and the water washed away the stains of defilement. So Christ is the "fountain . . . for sin and for uncleanness" (Zechariah 13:1). He gave Himself for the Church "that he might sanctify and cleanse it with the washing of water by the word, that he might present it to himself a glorious church, not having spot, or wrinkle" (Ephesians 5:26-27).

(9) The Tabernacle was the place where the guilty might freely go to the altar of atonement. And Jesus Christ "is the propitiation for our sins: and not for ours only, but also for the sins of the whole world" (1 John 2:2).

(10) The Tabernacle had inner chambers. And so it speaks of the deeper life and the fuller blessings into which those may enter who are willing to abide in Christ. "I am the door," Jesus says (John 10:9). "I am come that they might have life, and that they might have it more abundantly" (10:10). He is our Life, our Bread, our Light, our Altar of Prayer, our open Veil of access even to the innermost presence of the holy God.

(11) The Tabernacle was the place where the law was enshrined within the ark, ever covered by the sprinkled blood that proclaimed the sinner's acceptance. So Jesus keeps for us the divine law, then keeps it also in us by His indwelling life and presence, and so He becomes our perfect righteousness.

(12) The cherubim of glory in the Holy of Holies

were types of Christ's exalted glory, of His humanity crowned with the strength of the ox, the majesty of the lion and the loftiness of the eagle's flight. He is the pledge of our future glory.

All this and much more we see in this ancient object lesson concerning Jesus, of whom Moses and the prophets wrote. Jesus came Himself to fulfill the type with a fullness that He will yet enable us more fully to understand in every detail respecting the pattern in the mount.

God Fills the Tabernacle

SO MOSES FINISHED the work. Then a cloud covered the tent of the congregation . . . because the cloud abode thereon, and the glory of the LORD filled the tabernacle. . . . The cloud of the LORD was upon the tabernacle by day, and fire was on it by night, in the sight of all the house of Israel, throughout all their journeys. Exodus 40:33-38

That which is true of Christ the Head is also true of His body the Church. Among other points of instruction suggested by the Tabernacle in this connection, notice these:

(1) Like the Tabernacle, the Church has been planned by God Himself and is in no sense a human institution. It should in every respect be organized, constituted, built up and equipped according to the pattern that Christ has shown us. Jesus bids us to teach others "to observe all things whatsoever I have commanded" (Matthew 28:20).

(2) The Church requires the same divine anointing through the Holy Spirit on the part of all who, like Bezaleel and Aholiab, are engaged in her

spiritual upbuilding. Not the gifts of intellectual brilliancy, but the wisdom of the Holy Spirit and the enduement of His power are necessary. These alone can accomplish definite and eternal results. All else will wither and drift away in the fiery blasts of the great ordeal.

(3) The Church, like the ancient Tabernacle, should have her chief beauty within, not in costly decorations, but in the glory of the indwelling God and the exhibition of a crucified and sin-cleansing Savior. Without this she can only be what Israel's Temple was when the Master and the Shekinah departed and the avengers came with fire and blood. Without this His word can only be "Your house is left unto you desolate." Because the congregation at Laodicea were neither cold nor hot, Jesus declares "I will spue thee out of my mouth" (Revelation 3:16).

(4) Like the ancient Tabernacle, the Church should have her inner chambers for deeper teaching and closer fellowship. She must spend time in the Holy Place, in the light of the sevenfold lamp of truth, at the table of the heavenly bread. She must sense the sweet fragrance from the golden altar filling all the place with the breath of heaven; she must see the rent veil just beyond revealing and opening up to her vision the innermost chambers of heaven itself where shines the Shekinah of Christ's abiding presence.

(5) Like the ancient Tabernacle, the Church should be the repository of the world's true Light and the living Bread. The Church should be the light of the world and the stewards of the mysteries of

God.

(6) Like the ancient Tabernacle and Temple, the Church has her earthly and her heavenly life, the time of desert wandering and vicissitude, but the prospect also of a glory greater than that of Solomon's Temple. The day will come when the Lamb shall gather His redeemed on Mount Zion and the universe shall come to gaze on the glories of the New Jerusalem, prepared as a bride adorned for her Husband.

The Tabernacle a Type of Christian Life

What is true of Christ is true in the individual measure of each one of His people. "As he is, so are we in this world" (1 John 4:17). Let us not fear, therefore, to claim the fullness of our great salvation.

The first chapter in every Christian's existence is the dark, sad chapter of *condemnation*. This was vividly set forth in the ancient camp of Israel by the fire that ever burned without the camp. It suggests the wrath of God revealed from heaven against all unrighteousness of men. That fire consumed the offering to which sin had been transferred, and it must likewise consume all whose sins are not transferred to that burnt offering.

If Christ, in the place of the sinner, suffered this vengeance, how shall we escape if we dare to stand before God covered with our guilt and corruption? Our Lord has not quenched this fire but left it still burning outside the gate of the gospel for all who reject Him. "He that believeth not is condemned already" (John 3:18). "He that believeth not the Son shall not see life; but the wrath of God abideth on him" (3:36).

The next stage in the believer's life is *salvation.* We now enter the gate and stand within the court. We may freely come. There is no barrier, not even the fold of a curtain intervening. We hasten through the inviting entrance and stand before the smoking altar that tells us of the cross and the blood through which we have redemption from sin. We place our hand upon the head of the sacrifice, and we become partakers of the great expiation.

Next, the laver speaks to us of the Holy Spirit, whose power regenerates and cleanses from sin. We wash in its fountain and are qualified and authorized to enter into the inner presence, into the more intimate fellowship of the Holy Place.

Our Abiding in Christ

The Tabernacle also tells us of the next stage of Christian experience and life—*communion, consecration, sanctification* and *abiding fellowship* with Christ.

That inner chamber just beyond the open court is only for God's priests. How, then, dare we intrude? Thank God, we are all admitted to the place of priesthood if we will accept by faith "him that loved us, and washed us from our sins in his own blood, and hath made us kings and priests unto God" (Revelation 1:5-6). God has made us "a royal priesthood, an holy nation, a peculiar people" (1 Peter 2:9). So we may boldly enter in, but not until we have washed in that cleansing laver and sacrificed at the altar. We must accept His sanctifying as well as justifying grace. Even to Peter, who had been bathed, that is, justified, Christ said, "If I wash thee not, thou hast no part with me" (John 13:8).

Although we have boldness by the blood of Jesus to enter into the Holiest, we must come with "hearts sprinkled from an evil conscience, and our bodies washed with pure water" (Hebrews 10:22). Thus divinely cleansed, "let us draw near with a true heart in full assurance of faith" (10:22). Our great High Priest is standing within and sweetly saying, "I am the door: by me if any man enter in, he shall be saved, and shall go in and out, and find pasture" (John 10:9).

What pasture! There is the sevenfold lamp, which speaks of Christ and the Holy Spirit, our perfect light. He is the light of truth, the light that reveals Himself, the light of heavenly vision, the light that brings sight as well as light to our dull eyes, the light of guidance and direction amid the perplexities of life, the light of His continual presence, the light that will shine through us and from us as the light of men.

And the living Bread! The table with its 12 loaves, one for each of us, made from the finest of the wheat, ever renewed with each returning Sabbath! He is bread that not only nourishes both soul and body, but He becomes our perfect life and sustenance.

Not only is there bread, but there is frankincense like honey out of the rock—all the sweetness of His consolations as well as the strength of His life.

There is also all that is implied in the altar of incense. This includes a life of prayer and communion with God through Jesus Christ. That incense, together with the anointing oil, was the most sacred thing in all the Tabernacle service. It might not be imitated but was consecrated sacredly for the service of God alone. It was compounded of many ingredients, and some if it, we are told, was beaten very small, and then it was burned with sweet spices on the pure altar (see Exodus 30:34-38).

Even so the spirit of prayer must be born from above and cannot be imitated or counterfeited by mere human effort. It springs from the combination of all the circumstances of life and qualities of our Christian character. It is the flower of piety and the fragrance of the heart, distilled like perfume, indescribably delicate, pure and heavenly. Nothing is too small to enter into it and become an occasion for it.

The incense of prayer may be beaten very small and rise from a thousand trifles in our lives. But we may so consecrate it to God that it becomes a sacrifice of a sweet smelling savor. Our little trials and trifling ministries, laid on this golden altar, become to Him like the fragrance of the spring and the breath of Aaron's censer. He treasures them in heaven in "vials full of odours, which are the prayers of saints" (Revelation 5:8). But in order to be divinely fragrant, they must be set on fire by the Holy Spirit, the true Intercessor and Advocate on earth as Christ is the Advocate on high, making "intercession for us with groanings which cannot be uttered" (Romans 8:26).

The sweet incense of the Holy Place penetrated through the veil and filled the Holy of Holies. And so the spirit of prayer makes both earth and heaven one. The altar stood at the very entrance to the inner chamber. So when we are rapt in fellowship with God, we are at the gate of heaven and almost within the veil. We can hear the voices and catch the breath from those inner chambers. Happy are they who thus abide in Him, in the atmosphere of ceaseless communion and peace! The most trying place will be fragrant, like odors of heaven, and the most lonely spot will be a little sanctuary where all heaven will seem to be around us with its Almighty protection, its blessed companionship and its unspeakable joy.

The Holy of Holies

The innermost chamber in the Hebrew Tabernacle was the Holy of Holies. It speaks to us of heaven itself, the immediate presence of God and the *glory* that awaits us at His coming or at our translation. It tells us of a heaven not far off, shut out of our vision but near and open. The veil is torn in two from top to bottom, and the Holy of Holies sheds its light and glory all around us, even here.

Translation itself will scarcely be a change of companionship, although it may be of location. That inner chamber tells us of the place where our prayers can enter now in sweet incense and be accepted in His name. Our eyes can look through the veil and see heaven open and Jesus standing on the right hand of God.

There the sprinkled blood on the mercy seat is ever pleading for us and claiming our perfect and perpetual acceptance. There the ark within the veil, with the unbroken law in its bosom, is the symbol of the perfect righteousness we share with Him and in which we stand accepted in Him, even in the immediate presence of God. There the cherubim of glory are the patterns of the dignity and royalty that our redeemed humanity has already attained in Christ, its illustrious Head. That royalty we shall share in its fullness when He appears.

As we look through the veil, we know that our spirits, too, shall follow and be with Him where He is. The feet that tremble and falter shall walk through the gates of day, and the very body of our humiliation shall be like Him when He appears. We shall be changed into the image of His glory.

And all this we have even here, not only in vision and prospect but in foretaste.

> *The holy to the holiest leads,*
> *To this our spirits rise,*
> *And he who in His footsteps treads*
> *Shall meet Him in the skies.*

The Anointing of the Tabernacle

After the Tabernacle had been fully completed, according to all the patterns shown in the mount, it was solemnly dedicated to God, and the entire tent and its furniture were anointed with oil specially prepared according to the divine prescription and consecrated to this exclusive purpose. Then the manifestation of the divine Presence appeared upon it. The pillar of cloud spread its curtains above it, and the Shekinah glory took its place between the cherubim.

God filled the tent so completely that even Moses was not able to enter the Holy Place. Moses had simply and perfectly obeyed God's directions, and now God accepted his work and put His seal upon it.

This was symbolic of the anointing of Jesus Christ with the Holy Spirit and of the same anointing that comes upon every consecrated heart when it has obeyed the divine directions and presented itself a living sacrifice to God. God will so fill such a soul that there shall be no room for self and sin. This, indeed, is the true secret of sanctification and self-crucifixion: the expulsive power of the Holy Spirit's presence is the only true antidote to the power of self and Satan.

Henceforth the Tabernacle becomes the seat and center of the divine manifestation. We thus observe three stages of the visible presence of God in Exodus: (1) the pillar of cloud and fire that went before; (2) the presence from the mount; and now (3) the presence of Jehovah in the Tabernacle.

We trace the same three stages in revelation: (1) the Spirit of God manifested in the patriarchal dispensation; (2) the revelation of God under the law; and (3) the revelation of God in Christ, the true Tabernacle. "God, who at sundry times and in divers manners spake in time past unto the fathers by the prophets, hath in these last days spoken unto us by his Son, whom he hath appointed heir of all things, by whom also he made the worlds" (Hebrews 1:1-2).

We find God in the very first verse of Leviticus speaking to Moses no longer out of the mount or cloud but out of the Tabernacle. So we may find in Christ the continual presence and guidance of our covenant God.

"If a man love me," Christ says, "he will keep my words: and my Father will love him, and we will come unto him, and make our abode with him" (John 14:23). Let us only do what Moses did: yield ourselves fully and implicitly to the divine will and hand ourselves over as the property of Christ. When we do, we shall also be possessed and filled with a glory as divine as the Shekinah and as enduring as the life and love of God.

Henceforth, this event—the setting up and anointing of the Tabernacle—becomes a landmark of time. It was to begin the second year of Israel's national history; it was on the first day of the first month. The first year had begun with the Passover, but this forms the next great era of the nation's existence. And so the moment when we give ourselves to God and are anointed by the Holy Spirit, that moment becomes as important to us as the hour of our new birth. It is the beginning of months and years, from which all our experiences and hopes are henceforth measured.

Have we entered upon this second year? Have we begun it, like Israel, with the sacrifice of our beings in implicit obedience on the altar of God?

And have we received the descending fire and the abiding Comforter, henceforth to speak to us not from the heavens or even from the tables of stone, but from the inner chambers of His sanctuary in our hearts?

CHAPTER
3

The Altar and
the Blood

A ND THOU SHALT MAKE *an altar of shittim wood, five cubits long, and five cubits broad; the altar shall be foursquare: and the height thereof shall be three cubits.* Exodus 27:1

For the life of the flesh is in the blood: and I have given it to you upon the altar to make an atonement for your souls: for it is the blood that maketh an atonement for the soul. Leviticus 17:11

Forasmuch as ye know that ye were not redeemed with corruptible things, as silver and gold, from your vain conversation received by tradition from your fathers; but with the precious blood of Christ, as of a lamb without blemish and without spot. 1 Peter 1:18-19

The altar of burnt offering in the ancient Tabernacle court was the first object a person would notice upon entering the curtain that surrounded that ancient sanctuary. It stood just inside the entryway, accessible to all the people.

The altar of burnt offering was a large frame of wood covered with brass, sufficient to hold any offering that might be placed upon it. There was a fire constantly burning. The sacrifice was renewed every day, ever burning, ever smoking. The altar was ever blood-stained, ever open to any guilty Hebrew who might want to approach it.

It was so connected with the interior of the Tabernacle that everyone who went in had to pass it and had to take the blood from its sacrifices in order to be accepted in the Holy Place. Everything in that Holy Place was sprinkled with the blood. The high priest, when he entered the innermost shrine, must bring that blood or he would be smitten with death. Thus it had a very important part in the worship of the sanctuary.

Its place at the entrance of the Tabernacle teaches us that Christ's sacrifice, of which it is the type, stands at the very entrance of all our access to and communion with God.

Then again, the relation which it bore to the inner sections of the sanctuary, and that its blood was necessary in order to enter the inner shrine, shows us that Christ's blood is the only passport now to the presence of God, either in earth or in heaven. With it, we are accepted either on earth or in heaven to the very presence of God.

Further, it was accessible to the highest and the lowest, to every class of people. This indicates the fullness and graciousness of the great atonement that Christ has made for the sins of the whole world, sufficient for all, though effectual only for those who believe.

These are the chief lessons of the altar. There was nothing ornamental about it. It was unpretentious and ghastly looking. It was made of brass to bear the heaviest burdens and to sustain the streams of gore that bathed it and the ceaseless fires that burned upon it.

It was a place of suffering and blood, and it bore the constant mark of sin. So the Cross of Calvary, the death of Christ and the whole doctrine of the atonement have nothing very sentimental about them. The culture of man does not like it; the philosophy of the world would get rid of it if it could. But God has made His people prize the precious blood of Jesus Christ above all price and honor and love.

Passing on from this interesting object, we fix our attention on that of which the altar was the most emphatic expression: the blood. The blood runs not only through the Tabernacle and the altar, but we find it in all the types. It is particularly emphasized in seven places.

Blood on the Door Post

First, we find the blood on the door posts of the houses of the children of Israel. We find it sprinkling the lintels on that night when they escaped death by the destroying angel's wing. The blood kept them safe.

This may stand, then, for *redeeming blood*. Our lives were forfeited to death, but Jesus Christ redeemed us. He put His mark of purchase above our heads. "Worthy is the Lamb that was slain to receive power, and riches, and wisdom, and strength, and honour, and glory, and blessing" (Revelation 5:12). He has redeemed us; He has bought you and me personally. It melts my heart to remember that Jesus saw me in my ruin and took me and my responsibilities, suffered for me, loved me as a person and by His very blood bought me back from the bondage and penalty of sin.

Blood on the Altar

Second, we see this blood on the altar. It is spilt blood, shed blood. It is the blood of atonement. The blood on the door is redeeming blood. The blood on the altar is *atoning blood*, blood that washes out our guilt, blood that pays our penalty, blood that meets our obligations. It is Another's death instead of our death, a Life given instead of my life and yours. It has the significance of expiation and propitiation. Christ is the propitiation for our sins. He has borne our penalty for sin, and we are free.

Blood on the Leprous

Third, we see the blood on the person suffering from leprosy. Especially in Leviticus 14 we find the picture of the leprous person—that object of uncleanness and type of sin. We see the leper brought to the priest; we see the blood sprinkled upon him. We see the blood of the little bird touching his ear, his hand and his foot, in token that he is cleansed by the blood. We therefore have redeeming, atoning and *cleansing blood.* "The blood of Jesus Christ . . . cleanseth us from all sin" (1 John 1:7).

Jesus' blood heals from spiritual leprosy. It washes out our stains. It puts new life into our beings. The new leaves of spring push off the old leaves of the autumn past. Renewed blood in the body throws off the old, mortifying flesh and heals the wound. So the blood of Jesus Christ cleanses us from sin and keeps us clean.

Is His blood keeping you clean? This cleansing must be more than a mere theory or a thought. Can you say

Oh, the blood, the precious blood,
That Jesus shed for me,
Upon the cross, in crimson flood,
Just now by faith I see!

Fourth, we see the blood upon the book of the covenant. We are told in Hebrews that Moses took "of calves and of goats, with water, and scarlet wool, and hyssop, and sprinkled . . . the book" (9:19). The very commandments were to be touched with sacrificial blood, a type of Jesus' blood. It is the *covenant blood*. It seals the covenant, it pledges the promises, it answers for our failures, it guarantees our blessings. The blood of Jesus is on our Bibles, on the commandments, on all the promises. There is not a promise in the Bible but the blood of Jesus Christ has touched it, endorsed it, purchased it for us.

Fifth, we find the blood on the priests and on the vessels of the sanctuary. They were dedicated to God by blood. The right thumb, right ear and right toe of the priests were touched with the blood. So the blood consecrates us, as well as atones for and redeems us. It is *consecrating blood.* As it set apart the Tabernacle and the priest, it sets apart you and me. We dare not claim to be our own. If we dared, our very sense of honesty would make us blush to live for ourselves and then to look up to heaven and say,

"You have redeemed me, dear Father, and now I am going to do just as I have a mind to."

The very consciousness that we have been redeemed from death makes us realize that everything we are or have belongs to Christ. "Ye are not your own. . . . Ye are bought with a price" (1 Corinthians 6:19-20). So let our right ears be consecrated to hear only for God, our right thumbs to work only for God and our right feet to walk only where Christ has walked before.

Blood on the Mercy Seat

Sixth, we find the blood on the mercy seat. Within the sacred curtains, on that golden lid, under the flashing wings of the cherubim, amid the Shekinah glory—there was the blood. It was in the most sacred place of all.

The high priest carried it on the Day of Atonement and sprinkled it there before God's very eye on the mercy seat. It constantly remained there, pleading for the people, standing as the type of Christ's precious life. For the blood is the life that He not only laid down on earth but which He took up and carried into heaven. It is the life that He offers there at God's feet. He has presented it to God as the price and gift of redeemed man, and it pleads evermore for us before the throne.

So the heavens as well as the earth are dedicated with blood. This moment Jesus' blood is speaking there for us just as forcibly as it did at Calvary. We might express this as the *pleading blood*. It is Christ's life, it is Christ's death, it is Christ's great love, it is Christ's merits pleading for us evermore. He is claiming for us that which we claim according to His will.

During the Franco-Prussian War, in one of the regiments where discipline was very strict, one of the soldiers had disobeyed orders and was to be shot under sentence of court martial. He was in great agony of mind and, as the hour approached for the execution, the chaplain was sent to him. "Are you ready to die?" the chaplain asked.

"No," replied the prisoner, "I am not ready, but that does not trouble me. I am troubled about my wife and little children, thinking of their sorrow and of their future and of such a memory as they will have of me. When I think of the years of misery and sorrow they must go through, I cannot even think of my soul. Oh, I am so distressed! I am in despair!"

There was a fellow, a Christian man, well advanced in years, in the regiment who heard all this. Greatly affected by it, he stepped forward.

"I will tell you what I will do," he said. "I have neither wife nor children to mourn for me. It will be nothing to me to die. I would be glad to be with my Lord; let me die in your place." He talked to the chaplain and the commanding officer. They were moved by the man's sacrifice, but they did not know what to do. So they referred him to the superior officer, who could hardly believe the story.

"Do you really mean it?" the officer asked the Christian.

"Yes," replied the other. "There can be no question about it. That poor fellow is not ready to die. It would be eternal death for him. To me it would be but a quick translation to Jesus, whom I will soon see anyhow. I have not a friend on earth who would be the worse for it. Let me take his place."

The officer was both touched and perplexed. "I never had to decide anything like this before. I have no authority to make such a substitution. Suppose I defer the case for a day or two to lay it before the Crown Prince."

So the officer galloped off to see the Crown Prince, the soldier following, and brought the case before the prince. The Crown Prince was deeply moved.

"My brave fellow," he said, after he had listened to the proposal, "I have no authority to take the life of an innocent man. But I have the power to pardon. For your sake I will pardon the other man. Go back and tell him."

What a light that story sheds on our redemption. There was One who had a right to shed His blood, One whose life has been given. Christ, the admiration of every angel, of every saint, of the Father eternal, went down and walked through the world that the law might be honored, that He might show this wretched race that Someone could keep the commandments. Now He pleads by His merits for us unworthy sinners. And so He is represented in Revelation silently standing as "a Lamb [that] had been slain" (5:6). That is why no promise is too hard to claim. That is why faith can take all things in His name.

The Living Blood

Seventh, it is living blood. Jesus says, "Whoso . . .

drinketh my blood, hath eternal life; and I will raise him up at the last day. . . . He that . . . drinketh my blood, dwelleth in me, and I in him" (John 6:54-56). The blood of Christ is the life of our souls. It is the life of our bodies. It is *quickening blood*.

Jesus not only died for us, but even today He has fresh life to impart to us every moment. In medicine, blood from one person may be transfused into another and the patient will receive new strength and life. So Jesus can put His living blood into us.

Blood is not anything unless it is quickened by life. Pour that blood into a vessel, and it is putrid in a few hours. But pour it into someone's veins, and it is a magnetic force throbbing with life. "The life of the flesh is in the blood" (Leviticus 17:11). That is the reason Christ accentuates the blood. Oh, for the sacred flow, pouring His life more perfectly and constantly and fully into our weary souls, into our cold affections, into our weak purposes, into our weary nerves! There is quickening in Jesus, but it must be constantly claimed and kept by habitual trust and communion. This living, quickening blood is the life of our whole being.

We have seen the blood on the door—redeeming blood. We have seen the blood on the altar—atoning blood. We have seen the blood on the one suffering from leprosy—cleansing blood. We have seen the blood on the book—covenant blood. We have seen the blood on the priest—consecrating blood. We have seen the blood on the mercy seat—pleading blood. We have seen the quickening blood giving life to the soul and body, keeping us alive and strengthened through the life which comes from

God's heart.

May we echo back the words, "The precious blood of Christ!" *Lord, teach us more to know the sacred meaning of that blood and to say, "Thy blood is drink indeed."*

CHAPTER
4

The Laver of Water

A ND THE LORD *spake unto Moses, saying, Thou shalt also make a laver of brass, and his foot also of brass, to wash withal: and thou shalt put it between the tabernacle of the congregation and the altar, and thou shalt put water therein. For Aaron and his sons shall wash their hands and their feet thereat: When they go into the tabernacle of the congregation, they shall wash with water, that they die not.* Exodus 30:17-20

Jesus answered him, If I wash thee not, thou hast no part with me. Simon Peter said unto him, Lord, not my feet only, but also my hands and my head. Jesus saith to him, He that is washed needeth not save to wash his feet, but is clean every whit. John 13:8-10

The figure of water is universally familiar. Water is one of the most important and necessary elements in the physical world. We find it in the vast ocean, comprising by far the largest part of the earth's surface. We find it in our inland lakes and rivers that form such exquisite networks both of beauty and commercial value. We find it in the vapor of the skies and the dews that gather about the vegetable creation, preserving it from withering through our torrid summers. We find it forming the largest proportionate part of our own bodies.

Water is a figure of purity and refreshing, of quickening life and power, of vastness and abundance. Without it, life could not be for a single moment maintained.

Water in the Word

And so we find water in the Bible as one of the most important symbols of spiritual things. Away back in Eden there were four rivers that watered the garden and were, without doubt, types of the grace with which mankind was to be supplied. We find it again in the preservation of the life of Hagar and her son, supplied by the angelic agency. We find Moses striking water from the rock for the children of Israel, and we see them gathering around it with songs of joy and gladness. It becomes the source of supply in all their wanderings.

Water appears in the ministry of Elijah and Elisha. It brings healing to Naaman the leper and saves Jehoshaphat's army from destruction. In Ezekiel's vision we have the fountain of water where the filthy wash and become clean from their idolatries and the vices which flow from the temple of vision. Zechariah tells us of a fountain open for sin and uncleanness.

When we come to the New Testament, John's baptism was the symbol by which the Lord's reign was ushered in, and Christ carries the figure further to imply not only repentance but also regeneration and sanctification. "Except a man be born of water, and of the Spirit, he cannot enter into the kingdom of God" (John 3:5).

In His talk with the woman of Samaria, Jesus gave water an exquisite expression. In the service of the Feast of Tabernacles, He used the vessels with which men poured out the water as symbols of the water that He would give, even the rivers of water that He says shall flow forth from those who believe. From His own pierced body on Calvary's cross came forth a stream of blood and water for the healing of the nations.

The epistles of the New Testament are filled with the figure of water. Again and again we read of the cleansing and the purity that Jesus comes to bring to the world. And in the Apocalypse it appears in the vision of the finished work of redemption and the river of the water of life. The whole volume closes with this beautiful passage that points back to all the preceding figures: "Let him that is athirst come. And whosoever will, let him take the water of life freely" (Revelation 22:17).

And so this Tabernacle laver, of which we have read a description, stands just in the center of one of the most far-reaching of all the figures of the Holy Scriptures. In the Tabernacle and the whole Levitical ceremony, there were various uses made of water. The priesthood had to be set apart by cleansing. The leper had to wash himself with water and be shaved and sprinkled with blood and anointed with oil. The Israelites had also the water of separation with which those who had touched the dead had to be cleansed before entering the Tabernacle.

The Tabernacle Laver

This laver, or basin, was the second article of

furniture in the Tabernacle. It was formed out of the brazen mirrors of the women of Israel which they had brought from the land of Egypt, perhaps with excusable vanity, and perhaps without realizing that these belonged to their old life. When the Lord got them into the wilderness, He gently drew from them these memorials of their old life and consecrated them to a higher purpose. They were first melted and then cast into this basin, standing "with his foot," or pedestal, perhaps four or five feet high.

The position of this laver was just beyond the altar of offering. It was to be used by the priests alone, and it was to be used always by them before they entered the Holy Place. They were not permitted to go into God's presence with a spot or stain upon them. They had to wash before they could go in and offer their service. Neither could they go to the brazen altar with their offerings until they had washed in the laver.

Lessons from the Laver

Now that the picture of the laver is clear, let us gather the lessons.

The brass mirrors out of which it was made, and its probable ability to reflect the defilement upon the garment of the priests, suggest our first lesson. It is that God has provided for us in His Word and Spirit the influences by which we are to discover our own uncleanness and defilement. We must never forget that this inner monitoring is a major function of the Holy Spirit. All Scripture is given for doctrine (that is, teaching), but also "for reproof, for correction, for instruction in righteousness: that the man of God may be perfect, throughly furnished unto all good works" (2 Timothy 3:16-17).

God expects us to go to Him that He may reveal our shortcomings and blemishes, and we should be glad to see them even by painful methods. The Holy Spirit is the gentle reprover, quickly alerting us to evil. The soul, having an instinctive sensibility to sin, throws it off and applies the blood of Jesus Christ to cleanse from sin's very shadow.

Let us take God's mirror to show us where we fail. Let us not be so encased in the idea of being infallible and unreprovable that we shall fail to comprehend these lessons. Let us be glad, not that we made a mistake, but that that mistake has shown us something in which we are yet to be made stronger as we overcome. Let us thank God for this polished mirror and say as the psalmist said, "Cleanse thou me from secret faults. Keep back thy servant also from presumptuous sins; let them not have dominion over me" (Psalm 19:12-13).

Do not turn away from the Bible because it throws a reproving light on your soul. Do not shrink from prayer because it gives you a sense of unworthiness and guilt. Rather, remember that the laver, which shows the sin, is the fountain which will also wash it away.

Again, look at the laver as the fountain of cleansing. Water in the Scriptures is the chief symbol of the Holy Spirit. Blood tells us of the Lamb; water tells us of the Dove. God has sent one special Person, and His business is to make us clean, to purify and keep us spotless as His own unsullied wing. To this work God has given a divine Person, the infinite and almighty Holy Spirit, One filled with all possible resources for this work. Remember, it is His business; you are not imposing upon Him when you bring to Him your uncleanness. He has been sent, commissioned thus to fulfill the blessed redemptive work of our Savior Jesus Christ.

How precious it is to know that this Person is not away up in the heavens but is present in our hearts, ready to stoop down to our uncleanness. As Jesus stooped at the feet of Peter and washed his defiled feet with His own hands, so the Spirit enters our foul hearts and stays there until there is not a spot. Yes, the Holy Spirit is God's purifying messenger to us, bringing the water and the fire that will make us white as snow. Let us trust Him, let us obey Him, let us receive Him. And let us feel that we shall be without excuse for our failures if we do not.

Cleansing through the Word

The figure of water stands not only for the Holy Spirit, but for the Word of God, through which usually the Spirit of God works. We find it employed not only to denote the Spirit but the Word: "That he might . . . cleanse [the church] with the washing of water by the word" (Ephesians 5:26). "Now ye are clean through the word which I have spoken unto you" (John 15:3).

God's Word is the cleansing stream of the Spirit. "Sanctify them through thy truth: thy word is truth" (John 17:17). It first shows us our impurity, God's law, Christ's commandments. The sermon on the mount, the thousand directions of Christian duty show us where we come short; they show the path of purity.

But that is not the best. They give the promise of cleansing by which we are enabled to receive and retain His sanctifying grace. And so we read: "Having therefore these promises, dearly beloved, let us cleanse ourselves from all filthiness of the flesh and spirit, perfecting holiness in the fear of God" (2 Corinthians 7:1). And so Peter says in his second epistle: "Whereby are given unto us exceeding great and precious promises: that by these ye might be partakers of the divine nature, having escaped the corruption that is in the world through lust" (1:4).

Do you find any lack of purity? Take His promise and claim it. What can you want more than this? "If any man sin, we have an advocate with the Father, Jesus Christ the righteous" (1 John 2:1). There is remedy for any defilement. "If we confess our sins, he is faithful and just to forgive us our sins, and to cleanse us from all unrighteousness" (1 John 1:9). If you have some sin that is troubling you, bring it into the light and hand it over to execution. If you do, God is faithful and just. He will pardon you and, having pardoned you, will go to work and cleanse you—put the sin out of existence so it will no longer dominate you. He will cleanse you from all unrighteousness. So the Word is our laver and ever the efficient agent in the hands of the Holy Spirit.

What is the cleansing here typified? First, regeneration—the new nature, the new heart.

That comes after we trust in Jesus, after we come to the altar of blood and leave our sins there. Then the blessed Holy Spirit puts into us a new life and new spirit. That is the first step; it is the washing of regeneration.

Sanctification through the Word

But there is a more complete washing than this: the sanctifying grace of Jesus Christ. This is the complete and entire dedication of our whole beings to God by which we become His and His alone, and He becomes ours and fills us with His own nature and His own Spirit. He takes possession of our desires, our wills, our affections. He takes over all the faculties and powers of our beings and becomes the dominating, controlling, keeping power of our lives. He puts Christ, through the Holy Spirit, in our hearts.

It is not merely that we get a new heart and then go on struggling with a thousand elements of evil. Rather, our spirits and souls and bodies are dedicated to the Lord, preserved blameless unto the coming of the Lord Jesus Christ. Undoubtedly this is set forth in this ancient laver. It was not that the priests received a little cleansing; the laver meant that every spot was taken from them, for had there been one blemish, they would not have dared enter the Holy Place.

If this means anything, it means everything! If the Spirit and the blood of Christ can take away one spot, they can take away all. If they can keep you one moment, they can keep you a thousand years. If they can give you a single spark, they can fill you.

Suppose the priest had gone up and said, "I will wash off one little speck of defilement today, and some other day I will cleanse another." What would have been the consequence if he had ventured into the Tabernacle?

God says, "They shall wash with water that they die not." That single spot of sin would have been a conductor to receive the flash of divine anger. The Spirit of God requires of us, and brings to us, entire cleansing. The great hindrance to our receiving it is that we are afraid to believe so great a gospel. We are afraid to dare to take God at His word and to think that He is able and willing to do what He says.

"Then will I sprinkle clean water upon you, and ye shall be clean" (Ezekiel 36:25). One spot of sin in our hearts is like one spot of cancer in our bodies. We must be clean. I do not speak of our mistakes and misapprehensions, but I do speak of standing without any conscious, willful act of sin. We cannot go into the presence of God, we cannot have communion with God, we cannot have the peace of God if we are tolerating or consenting to anything in our hearts or lives that we know to be wrong.

You say, "It is too much to expect God to keep a man like that." God says that is the way He is going to keep us, and we have no business to belittle His keeping care and His precious redemption. Let us take Him fully, and while he may see in us ten thousand things we do not see, and while He will lead us ever to a deeper sanctification, this is a very different thing from tolerating evil. God accepts us as pure when we stand pure in all the light we have and do all we know of His blessed will.

Are you fully cleansed this day? Have you come to God's laver to see your whole self, feeling that everything is dependent upon your being right with God? Have you brought everything to Him? Do you with open face and heart take the cleansing water as well as the cleansing blood to wash every stain away? Do you believe He does it? And do you hear the Master say, "Now ye are clean through the word which I have spoken unto you"?

How touching it is that He said that to poor Simon Peter and to the very disciples who in 24 hours were to sin again! But He cleansed them and they were cleansed, and they believed it. Even if you should slip tomorrow, take His cleansing today. And if you take Him as Peter might have taken Him, He will keep you from stumbling and bring you to the presence of His glory at last with exceeding joy.

The Cleansing Is Continual

This leads us to another point: the continual application of the cleansing. Not only was it a single cleansing, but it was a very frequent, reiterated ceremony. The priests had to wash every time they went to the altar and into the sanctuary. This brings out a very precious truth: the Lord Jesus Christ, after He consecrates us thoroughly and fills us entirely, has still grace to fill us every day and grace to overcome all the ills and trials of life.

In John 13, we find Jesus using two expressions for cleansing, for the verbs are different in the original language. One describes a thorough cleansing. "He that is washed" (13:10). The word "washed" means to be thoroughly washed, that is, entirely cleansed—soul and body—and thoroughly sanctified. That person does not need to have the act redone.

But Jesus goes on to say, "He that is washed needeth not save to wash his feet." He will need to have his feet washed, to have the little stains of the passing earth, the little missteps that come a thousand times a day, removed. He does not need to be again saved and sanctified to God, but he needs a thousand rewashings from the transient defilements that had not entered his heart but had stained his feet. He who is washed needs not for his whole body to be plunged beneath the stream, but he needs to have the daily defilements removed. We may be washed in this larger sense, but if Jesus washes us not in this lower sense, we have no part with Him. Our communion is interrupted until we are cleansed.

This is the meaning of coming daily to the throne of grace and finding help in time of need. This is the privilege of the most consecrated believer. That blessed laver is open in our hearts continually, and the Great High Priest is ever there. He is there with the hyssop to sprinkle us and wash us over and over, even from the very shadow of the faintest contact that comes from the spirits of others or the atmosphere of the world in which we live.

And then what a comfort it is to know that the water was at the level of the priests. They did not have to climb up to it. It was right there, to be poured upon them. "Say not in thine heart, Who shall ascend into heaven? . . . Or, Who shall descend into the deep? . . . But what saith it? The word is nigh thee, even in thy mouth, and in thy heart: that is, the word of faith, which we preach; That if thou shalt confess with thy mouth the Lord Jesus, and shalt believe in thine heart that God hath raised him from the dead, thou shalt be saved" (Romans 10:6-9).

Who Was Cleansed?

We pass on, just for a moment, to glance at the persons who were to be cleansed. They were the priests of God, those who came to minister in the more immediate presence of God. They were not common people—the unsanctified crowd. They were God's consecrated ones, and they stand for that blessed place of privilege which all believers may occupy today. The priesthood of old meant consecrated service. And so this laver, this sanctifying Christ, this ever cleansing grace is given to us that we may use it in holy service.

There may have been a time when we felt this sanctifying grace was given to prepare us for the glories of heaven. This is not the end but the beginning of Christian service. The position of this laver was not in the far distant part of the Tabernacle, but just beyond the altar of sacrifice. First, the priests came to the altar, where they offered their victim, then they proceeded to the laver, where they washed away their stains. All this was before they entered into the Holy Place, the sanctuary of God, for His more immediate communion.

This is the meaning and place of sanctification. Oh, that we may learn where we stand! Christ does not withhold our sanctification until we get to the Holy of Holies. He gives it to us just after we have been pardoned, that we may enter His service, do His consecrated work and live a life of purity for His glory and the good of men.

And now, if it is true that God has provided all this for us, what a responsibility it places upon each of us! Look at it. The laver is not hidden behind those curtains; it is open to everyone, and so it is open to you. If you do not receive it, what will you say to Christ in the day of His coming, when He asks, "Friend, how camest thou in hither not having a wedding garment?" What can any Christian say who lives in any sin? He or she must be silent, having nothing to say. Let us be sure that we have not only come to the altar and the blood, but that we are washed with pure water. Let us be sure we are constantly keeping our garments unspotted from the world and cleansed in the ever-flowing tides of His love.

The Cleansing Is for Us

We have the altar that tells of His finished work, and we have the fountain that speaks of the infinite supply for all our needs. The specific purpose of the laver was cleansing. Have we received it? Are we walking with the Spirit of God?

We have trusted the Savior. Have we likewise trusted the Holy Spirit? We have received the blood. Have we received with equal fullness the boundless supply of His Spirit? We have prized His love demonstrated for 33 years as He dwelt among us as a martyr and an outcast. But have we recognized

His equal love shown for 1900 years as He makes His home with a vile and sinful race? He has been dwelling as one might have dwelt in a leprous hospital to cleanse away the vileness of our guilt.

I am ashamed whenever I think of that love and patience—ashamed that I have not loved Him more, and more perfectly yielded to His grace. This day take the Holy Spirit afresh! Let the vast and mighty floods pour into your nature, and as you go forth, go forth with the blessed consciousness that through all your soul God's waters flow, a stream of heavenly cleansing. That laver was ever full. So it stands today; there is enough for all.

And it comes down to the level of every one of us. Charles H. Spurgeon tells a quaint and interesting story of his early days. When he was a boy, he and his brother had two aunts whom they used to visit. When they went to see Aunt Margaret, they never received many cookies or good things; she had put them away on an upper shelf. But when they went to Aunt Jane's, they had all they wanted; she gave them the right of way and always put the cookies on the lower shelf.

How near Christ brings salvation! The law puts it away up in Sinai; even Moses could not reach it. But Christ has come to the level of the feeblest child and put salvation where anyone can reach it, like those ancient waters in the laver. The waters of His love and His cleansing are within your reach. Stand under them. Take that which God has brought so near and then go into His sanctuary and minister for His glory and for the sake of a sinful and dying world.

CHAPTER
5

The Light

A ND THOU SHALT MAKE *a candlestick of pure gold: of beaten work shall the candlestick be made: his shaft, and his branches, his bowls, his knops, and his flowers, shall be of the same. And six branches shall come out of the sides of it; three branches of the candlestick out of the one side, and three branches of the candlestick out of the other side: Three bowls made like unto almonds, with a knop and a flower in one branch; and three bowls made like almonds in the other branch, with a knop and a flower: so in the six branches that come out of the candlestick.*

And in the candlestick shall be four bowls made like unto almonds, with their knops and their flowers. And there shall be a knop under two branches of the same, and a knop under two branches of the same, and a knop under two branches of the same, according to the six branches that proceed out of the candlestick. Their knops and their branches shall be of the same: all it shall be one beaten work of pure gold.

And thou shalt make the seven lamps thereof: and they shall light the lamps thereof, that they may give light over against it. And the tongs thereof, and the snuff dishes thereof, shall be of pure gold. Of a talent of pure gold shall he make it, with all these vessels. And look that thou make them after their pattern, which was shewed thee in the mount. Exodus 25:31–40

Let your light so shine before men, that they may see your good works, and glorify your Father which is in heaven. Matthew 5:16

The two figures of light and oil are beautiful and interesting in their natural symbolism.

Light was the first created object of the natural world, and its chief glory. It is essential, in a great measure, to the existence of life. It is that which clothes everything with beauty and color. It is that which gives glory to the rainbow and the ruby. It is that which makes the diamond more than a little bit of carbon.

Light is that which makes the human face so full of loveliness. It is that which gives us everything beautiful in all the wonders of the natural world.

Nor have we only the light that comes from without. We have also the light that comes from within— the sense of sight and the power of insight that bring into our consciousness and perception the objects of nature around us.

We find this figure of light through all of God's Word. It was the most marked symbol of His presence. He appeared in the Garden of Eden in the light of the Shekinah. He appeared to Abraham in the lamp that passed between the pieces of the sacrifice. He appeared to the migrating children of Israel in the pillar of fire. And He appeared to Moses in the burning bush.

Jesus uses this figure of Himself. He claimed to be the light of the world, of His own children especially. The Holy Spirit is also the source of light. And the vision of the Apocalypse closes with the light that is brighter than the sun and a rainbow gathering up all its beautiful effulgence around the throne forever.

Likewise the figure of oil expresses many interesting thoughts. It is the source of artificial light. It contains in itself the elements of life and healing and, in contact with fire, the elements of light.

We find it employed for many other purposes than light. It was used in connection with the consecration of the priesthood and in healing, but it was especially set apart for the lighting of God's sanctuary. And it was specifically prescribed by God Himself and by the most awful sanctions guarded from being counterfeited. If anyone should endeavor to imitate or counterfeit it, he was to be cut off from among the people. Its ingredients were compounded together in some mysterious way for its sacred use, to light God's holy sanctuary.

The Golden Candelabra

The two figures of light and oil are combined in the golden candlestick described in Exodus 25. It stood within God's ancient sanctuary on the left, the first object which the priest saw upon entering the Holy Place. On the other side was the table of showbread. Near the inner curtain protecting the Holy of Holies was the altar of incense.

The candlestick was wrought of solid gold. A talent of gold [worth close to $1 million in 1985 money] was beaten into this piece of exquisite workmanship. It consisted of one stem or branch in the center with three lateral branches springing from either side. It was adorned with three kinds of ornaments: knops, flowers and almond-shaped bowls. The knops seem to have been fruit, probably pomegranates. Thus each of the branches running upon either side would be adorned with a flower of gold, then a pomegranate a little farther up the branch and then, on the top, the almond bowl containing the oil with which the light was maintained.

God was very particular in specifying these forms of decoration, and He told Moses to take care to make them after the pattern. All was of the same gold as the central stem. The flowers and knops and lamps were probably very elaborate and beautiful in their construction.

Then there were the usual tongs and snuffers. The lamps were daily replenished with oil by the priests.

Lessons from the Candelabra

The candlestick had many important spiritual lessons. God does not want His house now to be decorated with costly embellishments. Often where these are most lavishly employed, His house has been most dishonored. But He wants the pure light of divine illumination through His Word and Holy Spirit in our hearts and minds. The ancient candlestick was the token of these things. May God teach us something more about it today and make it more real to our hearts.

First, the candelabra teaches us that Christ is the light of the world. This figure of light is constantly appropriated by Him. He has given the light of reason to the human mind and it is He who brings light to the newborn soul. In the New Jerusalem He shall be the light thereof. If you want light in your soul, invite Jesus to come in. He will dispel the darkness, perplexity and sin and everything evil. "God is light, and in him is no darkness at all" (1 John 1:5).

Again, the candelabra tells us that the Holy Spirit is the instrument of light. While the light tells us of Christ, the oil tells us of the Holy Spirit. "The anointing which ye have received of him abideth in you" (1 John 2:27). He anointed Jesus of Nazareth with the Holy Spirit. "The Spirit of the Lord is upon me, because he hath anointed me to preach the gospel to the poor" (Luke 4:18). Jesus was called Christ because He was thus anointed.

And third, the golden candlestick stands not only for Christ and the Spirit, but it also stands for the Church and the Christian. It represents us as the reflectors of His light. It represents us as the sevenfold, complete light-bearers who give out this reflection to the dark world around us and so become the lights of the world. "Ye are the light of the world. . . . Let your light so shine before men, that they may see your good works, and glorify your Father which is in heaven" (Matthew 5:14-16).

These, then, are the special points of significance in this ancient type of light: Jesus Christ, our perfect light; the Holy Spirit, who sheds the light abroad in our hearts; and the believer and the Church of God who reflect the light on the darkness of a sinful world.

The Light Applied

Now let us gather some of the lessons that come from these lines of truth.

The light that God gives to us is all divine and in no sense human. This oil, as we noted, was not manufactured by any ordinary process or obtained from any apothecary's dispensary. It was made from materials divinely specified. It teaches us that the light we need does not come from man—not from the reasonings of the wise or even from our own soundest judgment. It comes to us from Jesus Christ and His precious Word. And all the light that God gives us in our heavenly journey must be divine.

Again, there was no light in the ancient Tabernacle but from this. There were no windows; the candlestick was the sole illumination of God's sanctuary. So with us: we have no other light but God. When we trust Him, we must wholly trust Him. "Trust in the Lord with all thine heart, and lean not unto thine own understanding" (Proverbs 3:5).

Have you this light? Have you taken all your ideas of things from the Bible and from the Spirit? Is your Tabernacle partly lighted by the golden lights and partly by the murky light of the world? Let us see that we have the light after the pattern on the mount. A great many Christians go astray here; they are not careful to have all their light from above.

Still further, we learn from the ancient candlestick that the light God gives us is a perfect light. It was a sevenfold light, and seven stands for completeness. There was not just one flame but seven flames, and they afforded all the light that was required. So God gives us light that has no darkness in it. When He leads us, we will find at last that it is always in the right path. And when He teaches us, we can lean our whole weight on Him, for He cannot fail. "God is light, and in him is no darkness at all."

Thus the Holy Spirit is called "the seven Spirits which are before [God's] throne" (Revelation 1:4). There is the spirit of peace, the spirit of sonship, the spirit of joy, the spirit of love, the spirit of trust, the spirit of prayer, the spirit of holiness, the spirit of power. These are all different forms of light, but they are all the same divine light.

God has a great many kinds of light. He has the light by day and the light by night. He is the light that guides and the light that glorifies. He is the light that shines with awful power upon our sins and makes us weep. He is the light that shines upon His own sweet face, His own precious cross and blood and lifts us out of our sin and makes our hearts happy in His joy. Sometimes the light shines from His truth, and sometimes it shines from the Spirit's presence in our lives:

> *Sometimes this light surprises*
> *The Christian while he sings,*
> *It is the Lord who rises*
> *With healing in His wings.*

And sometimes we cannot keep it in, but it shines out and sheds its glory on others—the sevenfold light of God in the heart.

Light Reveals

This light revealed the other objects in the Holy Place. It revealed to the priests the table covered with the showbread. The best thing about the light was that it revealed not itself but the bread. And so when this light comes to us, it is not that we will gaze until we are dazzled. Rather, the light comes to show us the Bread of Life, to show us how we are to understand the promises, to show us how we are to hold fast and be strong.

The whole plan of divine redemption becomes personal to us. The grace of Jesus Christ fills our whole beings and we wonder why we could not have taken Him more fully before, now that it seems so easy to feed on Christ and appropriate His promises.

You have the light; it is shining on the table. All is easy and plain.

I used to want the light in order to have a glorious experience. But I am glad now to get the light to show me how to live in Christ. If we looked at sunlight all the time in its full glare, it would be painful. But sunlight shows us our daily footsteps. It is to us the light of life. It is a dangerous thing, in the spiritual life, to be always wanting fireworks. It is far better to receive the light that shows us how to live.

The candelabra was to "give light over against it[self]." It was to show its own branches, as well as the other objects. It was to show that it was pure gold, that it was burning steadily. It was to show the beautiful flowers, the pomegranate fruit, the almond bowls at the top filled with oil for lighting the Tabernacle. "Over against it[self]."

And so, dear child of God, you want to have light to show that you are living right, to show the blossoms of your faith and hope, to show the pomegranate fruits that make your Christian life a blessing to others. You want to have light to show the almond bowls that hold the oil, not only to light your own path but the path of those around you. Does this light show you to be like Himself, beaten out of the same piece of gold and adorned with all the beauties and graces of the Holy Spirit?

Further, the candelabra required a daily replenishing of oil and a daily trimming of the wicks. Day after day the priest poured in the oil and used the snuffers to remove the charred parts of the wicks. And so God has to fill us with the Holy Spirit and use His snuffers. You and I can only shine with love when we are filled with love. We must be daily supplied with His oil, and we must see that the little hindrances are trimmed off. Have you taken away all the burned-out dross from your lamp? Have you the heavenly oil?

Only an Instrument

The candlestick did not have inherent light. It was only the bearer of the light; it only held the light, but the oil gave the light. And so you and I are not the light. Jesus Christ is our light, and we simply receive and give out Him.

This is the secret of all holiness. We are not light ourselves, and we are not expected to have light in our persons. But we have Jesus and show Him forth. He is the light that shines from our eyes, our manners, our tones. We are mere candlesticks to permit others to see Him. We do not stand before the people of the world and tell them that we are strong. We tell them that Christ is strong and that we use His strength. We do not tell them that we are wise. We tell them that Christ is wise and we simply use His wisdom. We have not faith but Christ has faith, and we draw from it moment by moment to glorify Him and not ourselves.

We are not love, and we never expect to love by our own impulses as God expects us to. But Jesus is the heart of love. Jesus is love itself, and Jesus is ours. His love is ours. We draw it in and give it out. We hold His love before the world and say, "He enables us to love as He loves, and yet without Him we should be a loveless lump of clay."

That must have been what the Master meant when He said, "Let your light so shine before men, that they may see your good works, and glorify your Father which is in heaven." We are to glorify God, not ourselves. People will not say, "What remarkable Christians they are; what pure spirits; what gifted minds!" Oh, no! But they will say: "How full they are of Christ; why cannot we be as they? They tell us they are as weak as we are, but God supplies their daily needs. Now, why cannot we do the same?"

That is what I mean by holding up the light of Jesus and letting it so shine before men that they will say, "This is the grace of God and we may have it, too."

Zechariah describes his vision of a candlestick, mentioning several points we do not find elsewhere. One of the most beautiful is that the candlestick was not replenished by a human priest, but by two olive trees that grew on either side. These two trees seemed to distill the very substance of their fruit and to press out the oil just as fast as it was needed, channeling it by golden pipes to the candlestick. This is a beautiful picture: the lamp not needing to be filled, but filling itself, because the pipes were always open. That is the way we can be linked with

God, so that, breath by breath, we shall be filled with Him.

There is one olive tree on one side—the Lord Jesus Christ—and on the other side the Holy Spirit, both pouring their lives into our souls and bodies and imparting themselves to us every moment. It is not a blessing that we get once in a while but a constant connection and communication.

So let us draw near to Him. So let us go forth to abide in Him. So let us have His light and His life. Then we cannot help shining, because we shall be just like Himself. And in His overflowing life we shall be a blessing to others, even greater than the blessing we receive.

Oh, may He come to us now and light up the sanctuary of our hearts until they shall shine like the chambers above! May He reveal to us the heavenly bread until we shall eat and be satisfied! May He open to our vision the golden altar of intercession and incense and, beyond, the rent veil, His own immediate, everlasting presence!

Amen!

CHAPTER
6

The Showbread

T HOU SHALT ALSO make a table of shittim wood: two cubits shall be the length thereof, and a cubit the breadth thereof, and a cubit and a half the height thereof. And thou shalt overlay it with pure gold, and make thereto a crown of gold round about. And thou shalt make unto it a border of an hand breadth round about, and thou shalt make a golden crown to the border thereof round about.

And thou shalt make for it four rings of gold, and put the rings in the four corners that are on the four feet thereof. Over against the border shall the rings be for places of the staves to bear the table. And thou shalt make the staves of shittim wood, and overlay them with gold, that the table may be borne with them.

And thou shalt make the dishes thereof, and spoons thereof, and covers thereof, and bowls thereof, to cover withal: of pure gold shalt thou make them. And thou shalt set upon the table shewbread before me alway. Exodus 25:23–30

And thou shalt set them in two rows, six on a row, upon the pure table before the LORD. And thou shalt put pure frankincense upon each row, that it may be on the bread for a memorial, even an offering made by fire unto the LORD. . . . And it shall be Aaron's and his sons'; and they shall eat it in the holy place: for it is most holy unto him of the offerings of the LORD. . . . Leviticus 24:6–9

For my flesh is meat indeed, and my blood is drink indeed. He that eateth my flesh, and drinketh my blood, dwelleth in me, and I in him. As the living Father hath sent me, and I live by the Father: so he that eateth me, even he shall live by me. John 6:55-57

On the right as one enters the Tabernacle stands the table of showbread, which these verses describe and whose significance they explain. The table of showbread stands across from and in the full blaze of the golden candlestick, which almost seems to shine for the purpose of revealing it alone.

It is a simple little table three feet long by half that width, and two feet three inches high, made of acacia (shittim) wood overlaid with gold.

Upon it there ever stand 12 loaves of unleavened bread, covered with finely powdered frankincense, offered before the Lord continually as a memorial. Every Sabbath these loaves are renewed, the old ones being eaten by the priests in the Holy Place, while the frankincense is burned before the Lord on the golden altar of incense.

This familiar type is so natural and expressive that there can be no doubt of its significance, and no difficulty in apprehending its beauty and fitness. As water and light are the natural symbols of cleansing and illumination, so bread as fittingly expresses the satisfaction and provision for the soul's deeper need that Christ supplies and the gospel reveals.

The same symbolism was present in the manna that fell for 40 years in the wilderness, and which, we are distinctly told, was designed to show them "that man doth not live by bread only, but by every word that proceedeth out of the mouth of the Lord" (Deuteronomy 8:3). In the bread of the Lord's Supper, the same element is preserved as the perpetual symbol to the Church of Christ's provision for His people's need.

Our Savior has claimed this symbol for Himself (see John 6:26-58). He shows how fittingly it expresses the real life that the soul can find only in His life and death. He shows how fittingly it expresses His living, life-giving Person of whom indeed it would seem to be not too much to say that all natural elements were made to be the symbols and foreshadowings. This is but the figure; He is the real Bread. His flesh is meat indeed, and His blood is drink indeed.

The Preparation of the Bread

There is much in this symbol that naturally suggests the deepest and holiest mysteries of Christ's person and work.

Bread is the fruit of the ground, which was cursed for man's sin. So Christ was born of a cursed and sinful race and came under that curse to become the life and support of the human soul. Bread is the offspring of death. The seed must be buried in the soil and die before it can produce the harvest that feeds the race.

So Christ Himself has appropriated this beautiful figure. He has taught us that, as the corn of wheat by dying grows into ampler life, so He was planted in death in the soil of Calvary. And from that dark sepulcher He came forth in resurrection life as the life of the world.

The grain from which bread is made must be crushed by the millstones. The dough must be kneaded in the baker's hand and baked in the fierce heat of the oven. So our heavenly Bread has been prepared and perfected under the crushing pressure and in the consuming flame of suffering. Is that pressing the symbolism too far?

In the natural world life is maintained not by direct impartation of power, but in the concrete form of bread. So the soul's life is not received direct from God the Father but in the Person of Christ.

The loaves had to be prepared. So the Bread of Life must be presented in a form in which we can partake of it—not wheat, not flour, not dough, but bread. Divine truth and grace must be adapted to human need.

All truth is not bread. Much preaching and teaching is but presenting ears of grain, sometimes with their barbs, beards and all. A divine revelation of God would not have been bread for a dying person. It needed to be concrete. It needed a Person who would gather up and concentrate in Himself all that God is to a lost humanity. It needed Jesus—truth incarnate, a personal, loving, suffering, sin-forgiving Savior.

There were 12 loaves, ample provision for all the tribes. So Christ is our all-sufficient Savior. Special provision is made for each tribe. Not one loaf for all, but personal provision for each one. That is the way Christ saves. Not all men en masse, but each one separately. "He . . . taste[d] death for every man" (Hebrews 2:9). He has a loaf for every one of us. There is for you a place as specific as if you were the only one for whom Christ died and lives. It is in the heart of God, in the work of Christ, in the thoughts of your Lord, in the prepared places of heaven. Oh, how touching this individual love of my Redeemer for me! How encouraging to me to claim my share! I am depriving none by receiving all; I am enriching none by declining anything.

The bread was unleavened. Not loaves, but cakes, because the process of fermentation was the symbol of sin and decay. The priests of God must eat incorruptible bread. The reason why so many are weak and sickly is that they are eating the leavened bread of human pleasure, pride and sin. "Labour not for the meat which perisheth, but for that meat which endureth unto everlasting life" (John 6:27).

The Offering of the Bread

Before the bread was eaten by man, it was first offered to God for seven days as a meal offering. So Christ's work of salvation was as much an offering to God as a provision for man.

We lose sight of this. There were necessities on the divine side as well as the human. There was a law dishonored; there was a love unyielded; there was a holiness offended by impurity and sin. There was a Father's heart deserving the love and obedience of a race He had created in His image.

Christ came to answer all these divine requirements even more than to meet human misery with full blessings. Christ came as man's answer to God as much as God's message to man. Christ came by His blood to meet the holy demands of justice. He came by His obedience to meet the claims of law. He came by His consecrated love to meet the longing of God's heart for love. He came by His purity and righteousness to satisfy the holiness of God and to do all this as a man.

In Christ God saw a Man canceling man's sin, bearing man's deserved penalty, receiving and obeying His law, loving and submitting to His will. He saw a Man yielding Himself a living offering of love on the altar of sacrifice and presenting a character so pure and holy that it was the reflection of His own. In Jesus Christ God was satisfied. He looked past those who had sinned and were sinning and saw only the one Man who stood for them. In Christ God accepts all. Christ's offering was an infinite satisfaction to God's blessed nature and character. It was the bread of God as well as that of man. It was a sacrifice to God of a sweet-smelling savor. And God's infinite being cried out, "My beloved Son; in thee I am well pleased" (Luke 3:22).

All of us who are in Christ are thus accepted through Him. His person, character and work are a substitute for ours, and we are accepted in the Beloved. Moreover, as far as His life and Spirit live in us, we too, like Him, are an offering to God, acceptable to Him. As man lives on God and finds in Him his life, so God lives in His children and has in them His life, His bread. So Christ describes the feast: "I . . . will sup with him, and he with me" (Revelation 3:20).

Therefore, we find our Savior always representing His work as done primarily for His father—

His Father's will, His glory, His pleasure. So also, before Jesus meets with His disciples or allows their communion, He must rise to His Father's presence and present His finished work. "Touch me not," He said to Mary; "for I am not yet ascended to my Father" (John 20:17). The Bread must first be offered on the heavenly table before it can be partaken of by the earthly children. The Head of the table, the Father, must first partake of the feast of salvation before His children can receive the cup of salvation.

But this once done, we find Him afterward not only permitting but commanding their touch, giving Himself to the probe of doubting Thomas. We find Him bidding Peter, and the other 10 on the Galilean shore, to that morning meal that was the type of the table now open to His children.

The Eating of the Bread

On the Sabbath day the old loaves were removed and eaten by the priest and new ones placed on the table. So while Christ is in the first aspect of His work an offering to God, He is in the second a provision for His people's need.

The spiritual meaning of this language none but a Christian can understand. And to a true believer, to a person who has felt the deep inner need of Christ and known His satisfaction, to one who is living in communion with the Person of Jesus Christ, it is unnecessary to interpret Jesus' promise, "I am the bread of life: he that cometh to me shall never hunger" (John 6:35). To one who has felt the crushing sense of sin and then the sweetness of assured pardon and peace by the Spirit's voice, there is no need to explain Jesus' statement: "I am the living bread which came down from heaven: if any man eat of this bread, he shall live forever" (6:51).

To the person who has felt the utter disappointment of human enjoyment and the bitter pain of human sorrow and then after all this has found the deep, satisfying sweetness of Christ's consolations; to the one who has found God's promises and commandments more precious than gold and more necessary than food, it would be idle to try to interpret and illustrate Jesus' words, "My flesh is meat indeed, and my blood is drink indeed" (6:55). Such an one has felt his or her way to the living Person of Jesus and knows what it is to have Him as an all-sufficient Savior, a perpetual Presence, a very present help and a Friend more near and loved than human affection can comprehend.

The showbread was eaten by the priests alone. They typified all true believers. So all Christians, all true believers and they only, can feed on Christ. No others can understand. No others desire such an experience. No others have either appetite or ability to appropriate Him.

It was a beautiful provision that, while the blemished and feeble were not permitted to minister at God's altar of incense, they were not to be hindered from eating the bread in the Holy Place. So although you may be too weak a Christian to do any useful ministry for Christ, although you may be too inconstant and unbelieving and cold even to offer acceptable worship, you are not thereby cut off from the provisions of God's house. Christ wants especially to feed and cherish the faint ones. Come and feed on Him until you are strong, until hands and feet and voice and tongue can join without blemish in His service, too.

The bread was eaten on the Sabbath, perhaps a type of the special provision God makes for His children on His own day. Here is the family table and the day of peculiar Christian nourishing. He who can afford to ignore it will find himself ill prepared for the conflicts and tasks of life. But it is almost as fatal an error to make this the *only* day of spiritual renewing as to neglect it altogether.

Every day requires new strength and grace. A person must have "daily bread" (Luke 11:3). The whole of the true believer's life is a Sabbath in the sense that he or she has entered into rest—rest from sin and self in Christ. In the enjoyment of His peace he or she can sing: ". . . I shall not want. He maketh me to lie down in green pastures: he leadeth me beside the still waters [literally, the waters of rest]" (Psalm 23:1-2). Have you learned to know this Sabbath? Have you found in Christ this living Bread?

The Frankincense

Frankincense was the symbol of acceptance. It was burned on the altar while the priests partook of the bread. It sent up its sweet perfume through all the Holy Place.

The first truth this suggests was the sweet acceptance by God of Christ's work. It is not only offered but accepted.

The second truth was the acceptance of the sacred meal of the priests as an act of worship. God accepted them in eating it. There is no more acceptable service you can render to God than to feed on Christ and rejoice in Him. Martha covered her groaning table with viands for her God, but Mary pleased Him more as she sat at His feet and heard His words. She fed on His life and love and worshiped Him by receiving what He gave.

The Table

The purpose of the table was to exhibit the bread. This is what the Church and ministry are appointed to do. What lessons we may learn from this table! It was simple. It had but one use: not to show itself but the bread. So the ministry is out of place when its brilliancy obscures the Savior. When the great Italian painter, Leonardo da Vinci, had finished his "Last Supper," he showed it to a friend. "What beautiful cups!" his friend exclaimed. The painter drew his brush over the canvas with a shadow of sorrow on his brow. He had failed. He had painted the cups, but not the Savior. Many a sermon is but an exhibition of pictorial skill in painting cups, and the Savior is in the background. May God make us like the table, only exhibiting the bread!

The table was for the purpose of holding forth the bread as an offering to God as well as for the priest's use. So the highest aim in all our ministry should be to hold Christ forth for God's glory as much as man's good. If you speak of Christ, if you live Christ so that God sees Him in you, it is heaven enough, even if no man rejoices. If I have held Christ up so that God is satisfied, even if you and others do not eat the bread, my ministry is not amiss.

Our first aim should be for God. The table, however, was meant also to hold the bread which the priests were to partake of. And so we must offer Christ to the world. But let us learn the lesson of the loaves and the frankincense. *Loaves*, not ears of grain, not lumps of dough. *Loaves*, prepared for the soul's present need—compact, concrete, warm, simple and in appropriate quantity.

And *frankincense*—attractive, sweet, appetizing— so that those who should will eat and live. Not loaves without the frankincense.

What is all this to you? Are you living on the bread of God or starving while in the Father's house there is bread to spare? The blight of the Church today is spiritual starvation. People are famishing on rationalism, socialism, sensationalism, on lifeless bonds and bank notes and unwholesome pleasures. "Wherefore do ye spend money for that which is not bread? and your labour for that which satisfieth not? . . . eat ye that which is good, and let your soul delight itself in fatness" (Isaiah 55:2).

Are you hungry? Christ stands at the door and knocks. He wants to enter, to spread a feast, to sup with you. Your salvation will be meat and drink to Him. Then He wants to have you sup with Him, on the rich blessings of grace now, and at the banquet of glory forevermore.

CHAPTER
7

The Incense

A ND THOU SHALT MAKE *an altar to burn incense upon: of shittim wood shalt thou make it. A cubit
shall be the length thereof, and a cubit the breadth thereof;
foursquare shall it be: and two cubits shall be the height
thereof: the horns thereof shall be of the same.*

*And thou shalt overlay it with pure gold, the top thereof,
and the sides thereof round about, and the horns thereof; and
thou shalt make unto it a crown of gold round about. And
two golden rings shalt thou make to it under the crown of it, by
the two corners thereof, upon the two sides of it shalt thou
make it; and they shall be for places for the staves to bear it
withal. And thou shalt make the staves of shittim wood, and
overlay them with gold.*

*And thou shalt put it before the vail that is by the ark of
the testimony, before the mercy seat that is over the testimony,
where I will meet with thee. And Aaron shall burn thereon
sweet incense every morning: when he dresseth the lamps, he
shall burn incense upon it. And when Aaron lighteth the
lamps at even, he shall burn incense upon it, a perpetual
incense before the Lord throughout your generations.*

*Ye shall offer no strange incense thereon, nor burnt
sacrifice, nor meat offering; neither shall ye pour drink
offering thereon. And Aaron shall make an atonement upon
the horns of it once in a year with the blood of the sin offering*

*of atonements: once in the year shall he make atonement upon
it throughout your generations: it is most holy unto the
Lord. . . .*

*And the Lord said unto Moses, Take unto thee sweet
spices, stacte, and onycha, and galbanum; these sweet spices
with pure frankincense: of each shall there be a like weight;
And thou shalt make it a perfume, a confection after the art of
the apothecary, tempered together, pure and holy: and thou
shalt beat some of it very small, and put of it before the
testimony in the tabernacle of the congregation, where I will
meet with thee: it shall be unto you most holy.*

*And as for the perfume which thou shalt make, ye shall not
make to yourselves according to the composition thereof: it
shall be unto thee holy for the Lord. Whosoever shall make
like unto that, to smell thereto, shall even be cut off from his
people.* Exodus 30:1-10, 34-38

The Scripture above is an account of the altar of
incense, the golden altar. It was the third article of
furniture in the sanctuary. It was at the far end of the
Holy Place, over against the costly curtains that
shielded the Holy of Holies. When the incense was
burning upon it, it filled both chambers and made
them fragrant with perfume.

The altar of incense was very simple in its construction. It was three feet in height and eighteen
inches in breadth, made of costly acacia (shittim)
wood and covered with a crown of gold around to
keep the incense from falling off. The incense itself
was most costly and precious, possessing special
sacredness, and preserved by divine sanctions from
being counterfeited or used for ordinary purposes.

What was the special symbolism of this little altar

in the ancient worship?

First, it represented Christ's intercession for us and also our intercession in the name of Christ. It is expressive of prayer and communion with God. There is something in the sense of smell that is perhaps finer than any other of the senses. The perfume that this sense appropriates is almost like the breath of nature, expressing the finer sensibilities of the soul of the natural world. And so fragrance has become the expression of the very outbreathing of prayer and love. The sweet breath of burning spices speaks of the sweet breath of prayer. It is the chosen emblem of the heart's homage to our heavenly Father.

But as the very highest example of prayer is the Son of man, so first it stands for the prayers of Jesus Christ. All through His life we see Him praying, and as His life is closing, it becomes the culmination of His ministry. As He crosses the brook Kidron, He is in prayer. In the garden He prays. On the cross He prays. As He passes from earth, we know He is exalted at God's right hand, there to engage in the unceasing work of intercession, for He "ever liveth to make intercession for [us]" (Hebrews 7:25).

So, on this ancient altar, the ascending incense continually filling the sacred chamber was the type of Christ. His whole being was one breath of love, sweetness and consecration to God, as well as a remembrance of us, His dear children.

And, expressive of His intercession, the altar of incense fittingly becomes the example for our imitation and the pattern of our prayer, of our communion with God. It is a pattern of that sacred place where "spirits blend, and friend holds fellowship with friend," where every heavenly blessing can be brought down by the prayer of faith.

In connection with this altar, let us think of these two things: of Christ who at God's right hand is remembering us and on His uplifted hands presenting our names for acceptance with God, and of our spirits' communion with God.

Sweeter than the air of that ancient Tabernacle may your whole spirit be baptized, your inmost being perfumed with devotion until God will come down to dwell in the delightful place. May it be, as we read in the Revelation, that the prayers of the saints are gathered in vials as sweet odors with which God refreshes even His own heart amid the glories of the celestial courts.

Lessons from the Incense Altar

All the lessons connected with this ancient altar of incense may be applied to these two thoughts—Christ's intercession for us, and our prayers and intercessions in His name.

1. The altar was of incorruptible wood and incorruptible gold. Our Lord has a twofold nature. He is divine, and yet He has a perfect humanity. The wood represents His humanity, the gold His divinity. So the believer has a human and a divine nature; human, and yet a partaker of the divine nature.

If you have received the cleansing and sanctifying nature of the Lord Jesus Christ, you may claim participation in this double life. It is, indeed, a great mystery. It would be an awful blasphemy if it were not founded on God's Word. But every Christian is born of God. His new nature, like that acacia wood, is incorruptible. And like that more precious gold, he possesses the very life and spirit of Deity Himself.

2. The altar was the highest object in the Tabernacle, several inches higher than the table of showbread and higher than the laver or the brazen altar of sacrifice in the Tabernacle courtyard. So prayer is the most exalted ministry in the universe. A person on his or her knees is more elevated than at any other time.

3. This altar was crowned. We observed earlier how the table of showbread was crowned. So was this altar. Christ as our High Priest is a crowned Priest. He is not pleading with uncertainty but with victory. He is not saying, "I wish it might be"; but, "Father, I will that they also, whom thou hast given me, be with me where I am" (John 17:24). "Father, I will that Peter's faith fail not. Father, I will that this child of mine overcome today." It is a royal priesthood, and it is for you. Jesus' intercession is effective.

You, too, have a royal priesthood. You can go into the presence of God, crowned. You can feel you are so near the King that you can ask special favors, and thus your prayers will be a constant ministry for others. Oh, that you might realize this and, like Esther before Ahasuerus, know that you have the power to claim blessing for those who have not the power!

Lord, help us to be true to this ministry, this authoritative asking, this crowned priesthood of which the Master says, "What things soever ye desire, when ye pray, believe that ye receive them, and ye shall have them" (Mark 11:24).

"Thus saith the Lord, . . . concerning the work of

my hands, command ye me" (Isaiah 45:11). "Whosoever shall say unto this mountain, Be thou removed,
and be thou cast into the sea; and shall not doubt in his
heart, but shall believe that those things which he
saith shall come to pass; he shall have whatsoever he
saith" (Mark 11:23). It is the royal scepter of intercession. Jesus says to us: "I have . . . ordained you,
that ye should go and bring forth fruit, . . . that whatsoever ye shall ask of the Father in my name, he may
give it you" (John 15:16). He expects you to triumph
in this ministry, to take up the crown of prayer that
He wears and shares with you.

To All Peoples

4.   Another distinction with this altar was the
horns. It had four—one on each corner—pointing to
the four quadrants of the compass and to the different camps of Israel. There were four great camps,
and so the prayer of our Lord reaches north and south
and east and west. It is for all His people and for all
the ages of His Church, and for all the quarters of the
globe where they may be. Nowhere can we be iso-
lated from His sympathy and His victorious help. It is
pointing this very moment to your need and saying,
"Father, deliver! Father, give the victory! Oh, think
of that horned altar, the symbol of victory over Your
enemies, and claim triumph for us!" Rise up, and
praise and trust Him for it.

So should it be with our prayers. We must be very
wide in the circle of our prayers. Keep out of the ruts
of selfishness.

We must enlarge our souls. A brother said, "I have
found the outlet—to pray for others." When your

heart is pent up and likely to burst, this is the outlet—
pray for someone else. Let your sympathy be very
wide. Let it have its objects in every land and on
every continent. You can win people in Africa as
well as here, and if every moment of your life is spent
in prayer, you shall find when you get home that you
have multitudes of trophies.

Prayer is the greatest of our ministries. It is much
greater than preaching. It is the best thing we can do
for God. I remember a service in which I saw no
fruit. I had prayed much for that particular congregation and yet it seemed in vain. Then later, in a
rather tired moment, I took up some letters, and I
found wonderful testimony from that meeting of one
and another who had been saved there or had gone
from that place stricken with a sense of guilt. Some
had spoken to others, and they, too, had been saved.

In the work of the gospel there is no power but
God. We must trust Him and expect the things we
ask. The great question is, What is God going to do?
It is a very little matter how persons will be im-
pressed by what a man may say, whether it seems
very bright or very dull. But how is the Holy Spirit
going to make these persons feel their need and
arouse them to victory? It is the Holy Spirit claimed
by prayer who is the secret of success.

5. There were rings on this golden altar by
which it was carried from place to place. I am glad
of that. It was not stationary so that people had to
make pilgrimages to it, but it went with the camp. So
it is with us. There is not a place on the journey
where our altar does not come. We can turn Jacob's
stony pillow into a ladder up to heaven. Do you carry

your altar with you? Have you rings in your altar of prayer? Do you take it with you to business? Do you take it with you on your visits and holidays and picnics? God expects you to be just as near Him on your holiday as you are on Sunday. Have you the rings? And have you the staves in the rings? Can you pray anywhere? Have you learned to let the curtains down and be alone with God at any time?

6.　Note that the fire on the altar was always burning, and the sweet spices, too. The incense was continually rising. And so the Lord Jesus is all the time praying for you. You slept all the night, but all the time He was praying. You awoke, and He was there. It is one of the sweetest experiences of my life to awake and feel Him near. It is delightful when He brings something to my mind, something that I would have forgotten, and to realize that He is ever remembering me.

And how often our hearts get oppressed with the burden that presses us to pray! It is Jesus praying for us. The fire is burning, the incense is ascending. We may not say words all the time, but the incense can rise. In the world of nature, evaporation goes on all the time. We can see the mist in the morning but not at noon, yet there is twice as much evaporation then because there is more heat. We do not see it. So we can all the time be breathing up to God the homage of our hearts.

You ask, "How can I put my whole heart in my business and pray?" You can. I used to be very fond of gardening. I could work in the garden and yet smell the roses; they did not keep me from my gardening. I had my sweet flowers every second; they did not hinder the work. So you can be busy all the time and have the breath of heaven. It will not hinder you. It is like working in a perfumed room, every sense exhilarated. It is something deeper than prayer. It is communion.

It is like the mother and child, or friends sitting together as I have seen them for hours. Not a word passes, yet they feel each other's presence. So Christ is with you. You do not talk, but there is communion. This is the right state of heart to live in. It will make the shabbiest house a sweet place. It will put zest in your work for the Lord. Even in the most disagreeable work you can sing. It will make the kitchen a palace. Even as you encounter sin, God's presence will be like a heavenly disinfectant. You can work in any atmosphere.

Sometimes when I would go down to our mission work I felt as if I would choke from the evil atmosphere around me, the filthiness of men's hearts and the grossness of sin. But the golden altar was with me and the sweet incense of prayer. I was lifted above the depressing atmosphere and the desert blossomed as the rose.

There Was Fire on the Altar

7.   We read that there was no incense without fire. So Christ's intercession for us had to be preceded by the fire of suffering. It is not prayer that saves us, but death. It is because Christ died to make atonement for sin that now He can deliver His blessings. Prayer is not enough. There must be fire. All the seclusion of the Buddhist or the prayers and scourgings of the ascetic will not save without the

fire. So the fire of suffering was the first preparation for the intercessory work of the ancient priest.

This fire also represents the Holy Spirit. The Holy Spirit is called the Spirit of prayer. It is the Spirit who brings down to our hearts the desires that God would make us feel. It is He who prompts in our souls the inclination and the sense of need.

How easy it is to pray when we are carried on His wings, when our souls float out on the breath of God! We feel that God must give, because God Himself has already asked! It is He who breathed it up to heaven, and He will pour it back. Blessed Spirit of prayer! Do not discourage Him. Listen, and He will come and come until He will do all your praying, and it will be divine. Blessed prayer! It will not be the cold form of nice words but the burning incense of a heart that cannot keep the petitions back.

8. We come to the most beautiful of all these symbols: the incense itself. It consisted of four parts. Three we do not know, one we do. The frankincense is the gum of an Arabian tree and an object of commerce. The other three are unknown. And so we are taught that in the intercession of our Lord, there are some things we do not know. There is His human nature that we understand, which may be represented by the frankincense, but there are the divine things like the unknown spices. We cannot measure their depth or height.

In our prayers there are things we know and things we do not know. There ought always to be definiteness in our prayers. Often we may know what is according to His will and expect it. But perhaps the largest part of our praying in the Holy Spirit will be like the three unknown spices: we cannot tell just what the cry means. But we shall be conscious of a cry that cannot be articulated. We shall feel that God knows it. It is articulated in His ear and He will give us the answer and show us in due time.

This may help you to understand many of your perplexing burdens of prayer. Sometimes God lets you know, but many times you cannot know. There has been that unutterable outreaching that seemed incapable of interpretation or understanding—a prayer you did not comprehend and did not need to know. Sometimes you feel God is averting some danger or saving some dear one or blessing some special work or carrying someone through a crisis. There are days when you feel if you let go, something will give way and be lost to the cause of Christ forever.

On the battlefield the foot soldiers may not understand the plan of action, but the commanding officer does, and when the battle is over the foot soldiers, too, understand it. So let us trust everything to our Captain. Although we do not know it all now, we shall understand hereafter. And God will bring us many an enraptured trophy and say, "He or she was the one born of your prayer." He will show us many a glorious issue of His work and say, "That was what you held up to me in prayer!"

God Is God of the Small Things

9. But there is this most beautiful facet I want you not to miss. God says of this aromatic mixture, "Beat some of it very small, and put of it before the testimony in the tabernacle of the congregation,

where I will meet with thee." Some of these grains of frankincense and galbanum were to be pulverized, then they were to be burned in the little grate and go up so sweetly that not one grain was lost.

Be assured there is no little petition, there is no little heartache, there is no little desire too small for Jesus to pray about or for you to pray about! That finely powdered incense symbolizes the little needs of your life, and yet each one is gathered by Jesus Christ in its minutiae and presented to the Father with the same care as though it were the fortunes of a kingdom. It cannot be insignificant; nothing that is passing through your thoughts is too small for Christ to pray about, or for you to go to God about. That is the way to make God familiar and to make common things real—by burning them on God's altar. God help you to bring the little things of life to His mercy seat.

10. Finally, the position of this altar was significant. It was between the two chambers. It was in the earthly, but it touched the veil, and its incense went into the heavenly. Those two chambers represented earth and heaven. The outer chamber was the believer's life in its earthly experience, and the inner chamber was the Holy of Holies beyond.

Prayer brings us to the very gates of heaven. When we are at the mercy seat, we are partly on earth and partly in heaven. Our prayers are in heaven already, and we are breathing the very atmosphere of heaven. It is all open; it is one blessed chamber where we have fellowship not only with our brethren below but with the hearts that wait for us above. So it was that while Jesus was praying, He was transfigured before

His closest disciples. While Stephen was praying, his face became like the face of an angel. And while you wait upon your Lord you shall change your strength: you "shall mount up with wings as [an eagle; you] shall run, and not be weary; and [you] shall walk, and not faint" (Isaiah 40:31).

The effects of this incense and of this altar were very beautiful. We have a description of them in Revelation 8, where we read of the angel who "came and stood at the altar, having a golden censer; and there was given him much incense, that he should offer it with the prayers of all the saints upon the golden altar which was before the throne" (8:3).

It is an old interpretation that this angel was the Lord Jesus, that the incense was the prayers of the saints and His intercessions mingled with the prayers of the saints. And the meaning is that when we send up our prayers before God, although we may feel there is much that is unworthy in them, yet the hands of the blessed Angel take them before they get to God. He drops from them every grain of impurity and only keeps that which is acceptable to the Father. With that He mingles His own intercession, breathes His own breath upon our purified petitions and with His holy hands offers them at His Father's feet. Then there comes the sweet answer of God's love, and we are accepted in the Beloved.

True Fire or False?

There is an awful contrast here between the true fire and the false fire that some of the priests presumed to bring to God. The consequence of the "strange fire" (Leviticus 10:1) was most fearful vengeance. And anyone who should counterfeit this perfume was to be cut off from his people. To counterfeit was death then; to counterfeit is death still.

Are you approaching the most holy Presence through the blood of Jesus? Or are you approaching with your own natural thoughts, your self-righteousness, your self-will? If you are bringing strange fire, it will be death. Are you counterfeiting God's holy incense? Are you letting feeling, sentiment, delightful music, sacred eloquence, poetic rapture or anything but the Spirit of God take the place of true devotion? If it is not in the name of Jesus, it is strange fire! It is counterfeit, and it is death.

There are ministers who use the ministry of God to tickle the fancy of audiences, who play with people's sentiments, who use sacred song and holy worship and the very church of God for mercenary purposes or personal gain. God said, "Whosoever shall make [incense] like unto that . . . shall be cut off from his people."

Are you coming to God through any other means than Christ alone? Are you looking for salvation in any other way than through His death? "There is none other name under heaven given among men, whereby we must be saved" (Acts 4:12).

Are you living this life of communion with God? Do you know this heavenly way? Have you ever experienced these divine communings? Is this figure of frankincense anything to you? Is your heart like this sweet place? Or is it a place of rank and unclean things, with the smell of earthly carrion and the unclean sewage of your own sins?

Oh, come to God to cleanse you, and in the place where dragons crawl and serpents find their slimy haunts He will dwell. The wilderness and the solitary place shall blossom as the rose! Your poor heart shall become like the very gates of heaven, where angels will love to gather, where the Dove of Peace will fold His wings and rest. And you shall say even in the darkest hour, "This is none other but the house of God, and this is the gate of heaven" (Genesis 28:17). Have you this little perfumed sanctuary? "I will be to them as a little sanctuary," says God (Ezekiel 11:16).

Some of us, as we walk through this wilderness, are sweetly conscious that we carry our tent along. It folds around us every hot midday, and every dark night the lamps are lighted within, and the air is all sweet with the very breath of heaven. "Blessed is the man whom thou choosest, and causest to approach unto thee" (Psalm 65:4).

Walk in the light of the Lord until He shall say, "Come, ye blessed of my Father, inherit the kingdom prepared for you" (Matthew 25:34). Then you will enjoy not the shifting tent of the wilderness but the palace of the King!

CHAPTER
8

The Holy of Holies

A ND THEY SHALL *make an ark of shittim wood: two cubits and a half shall be the length thereof, and a cubit and a half the breadth thereof, and a cubit and a half the height thereof. And thou shalt overlay it with pure gold, within and without shalt thou overlay it, and shalt make upon it a crown of gold round about.*

And thou shalt cast four rings of gold for it, and put them in the four corners thereof; and two rings shall be in the one side of it, and two rings in the other side of it. And thou shalt make staves of shittim wood, and overlay them with gold. And thou shalt put the staves into the rings by the sides of the ark, that the ark may be borne with them. The staves shall be in the rings of the ark: they shall not be taken from it. And thou shalt put into the ark the testimony which I shall give thee.

And thou shalt make a mercy seat of pure gold: two cubits and a half shall be the length thereof, and a cubit and a half the breadth thereof. And thou shalt make two cherubims of gold, of beaten work shalt thou make them, in the two ends of the mercy seat. And make one cherub on the one end, and the other cherub on the other end: even of the mercy seat shall ye make the cherubims on the two ends thereof. And the cherubims shall stretch forth their wings on high, covering the mercy seat with their wings, and their faces shall look one to another; toward the mercy seat shall the faces of the cherubims be.

And thou shalt put the mercy seat above upon the ark; and in the ark thou shalt put the testimony that I shall give thee. And there I will meet with thee, and I will commune with thee from above the mercy seat, from between the two cherubims which are upon the ark of the testimony, of all things which I will give thee in commandment unto the children of Israel. Exodus 25:10-22

For there was a tabernacle made: the first, wherein was the candlestick, and the table and the shewbread; which is called the sanctuary. And after the second veil, the tabernacle which is called the Holiest of all; which had the golden censer, and the ark of the covenant overlaid round about with gold, wherein was the golden pot that had manna, and Aaron's rod that budded, and the tables of the covenant; and over it the cherubims of glory shadowing the mercyseat. Hebrews 9:2-5

We need not dwell on the form and dimensions of this remaining part of the Tabernacle. You will understand that the inner Holy of Holies was a perfect cube, separated from the Holy Place by the costly and gorgeous curtain, or veil. It contained the most beautiful workmanship of any part of the structure. It was lined on three sides with gold and adorned with the most elaborate embroideries. It contained a single article of furniture—a little chest called the ark, between two and three feet high and not quite four feet long. It had within it the two tables of the law. For a time it also contained two other articles of typological interest—the pot of manna preserved from the desert and the rod of

Aaron that had been the budding symbol of his divine and authoritative priesthood.

The ark had also carrying poles that fit through gold rings on its four corners. Atop the ark was the propitiatory, or mercy seat, of solid gold, stained by the blood that was brought in by the high priest once a year. Above this mercy seat rose the figures of two cherubim. And between their arched wings was the visible Shekinah—the presence of God, which ever hung there and which seems to have spread out into the cloud that guided Israel and sheltered them in their wilderness journey.

This Holy of Holies was the principal point of interest in the Tabernacle. It was the presence chamber of God. It was visited only once a year by the high priest, on the Day of Atonement. When he entered he carried the names of the people of Israel on his breast and shoulders and made reconciliation for their sins.

This Holy of Holies has come to represent the highest and deepest communion of the soul with God. This inner chamber is the secret place of the Most High, where we can now enter through the blood of Jesus. Opened to all by the Savior's death, it sheds its light and glory on all our lives. It is yet more emphatically a worthy and glorious type of that which is still unrevealed—the glory of the eternal world. It is a type of the light of His presence who is Himself the glory of the city that has no need of the sun, for the Lamb is the light thereof.

The Veil Is Gone

This veil represents the obstructions that came

between the soul and God in the Hebrew dispensation, obscuring the full revelation of God's presence and grace. And it represents, on the other hand, the removal of those obstructions and the revelation that has since come through the finished work of Christ. So it stands for both separation and revelation, representing the things that once kept us from God and then the way in which we may come to God in the most intimate fellowship.

We are told that this veil was the flesh of Jesus Christ (Hebrews 10:20). When His flesh was put aside by the cross, this veil was "rent in twain" (Matthew 27:51), and the Holy of Holies was opened to view and to the entrance of God's believing and trusting people.

Now I cannot but believe that this was a type also of the entire fleshly life of the people of God, and that the death of the Lord Jesus Christ is a type of the death into which we enter when we consecrate ourselves to God. And the removal of the veil, which was withdrawn through His death, represents the death that comes to us when we die with Christ and rise into newness of life.

As long as your flesh is indulged and suffered to remain, there is no way for you to enter into the Holiest of all. You cannot see it. The old nature hinders your seeing the glory of God. But when self dies, the veil is torn in two, the glory of God is revealed, and the voice of the Spirit says: "Having therefore . . . boldness to enter into the holiest by the blood of Jesus, by a new and living way, which he hath consecrated for us, through the veil, that is to say, his flesh, . . . let us draw near with a true heart in full assurance of faith" (Hebrews 10:19-20, 22).

Everything, therefore, that helps you to die to self helps you to live in Him and is the opening up of the glory of God to you. If you can say, "I am dead with Christ" and "I am risen with Christ," you can understand something of the apostle's language when he prays "that Christ may dwell in your hearts by faith; that ye . . . may be able to comprehend . . . the breadth, and length, and depth, and height; and to know the love of Christ, which passeth knowledge, that ye might be filled with all the fulness of God" (Ephesians 3:17-19).

Has the veil been rent in twain for you by the death of self? If so, your heart is a holy Tabernacle, and there is no barrier there between you and the throne of God.

The Mercy Seat

Let us step in reverently and next look at the mercy seat. This is the golden lid of the ark of the covenant. The lid is the mercy seat. It is the same gold that was wrought into the cherubim above it. They are all of one piece. Now *mercy seat* means literally in Hebrew a bloody covering. It hides something; it covers something that otherwise would be unfit to see.

What did this mercy seat cover? In that ark was the record of Israel's sins. In it was the broken law, every line of which called to heaven against the nation, every line of which was a witness of their sins.

Suppose it was your sins. And suppose there was no lid on the ark—that it was all open. And suppose that the stony table was witnessing against you forever. And now, see above you the awful Shekinah eye, looking on the record. Would you not want something to hide your sin from His sight?

And what if you saw an angel's hand bring a lid of pure, imperishable, impregnable gold and clamp it down over the record of your sin? What if that angel sprinkled the blood that could answer heaven for your sin and say to the holy God, "Punished, pardoned, ransomed because of Jesus"? Would not that be a glorious covering? So it is! And so David sings, "Blessed is he whose transgression is forgiven, whose sin is covered" (Psalm 32:1).

Covered is the same word used for mercy seat. Again we read, "He hath not beheld iniquity in Jacob, neither hath he seen perverseness in Israel" (Numbers 23:21). Why? Because it was covered. Oh, this is the meaning of salvation—covered forever by the blood of Jesus, by the righteousness of Jesus!

And so this mercy seat has come to represent God's mercy. But further, it has come to mean the privilege of communion and of fellowship on the ground of Christ's atonement and intercession.

The Lord says, "There I will meet with thee, and I will commune with thee from above the mercy seat." There is nothing now between us and God— no guilt, no sin, no fear. We can bring our desires and our needs, and we can come again and again, for there is no veil now. The veil is put aside, and the voice of love is saying, "Let us draw near . . . in full assurance of faith" (Hebrews 10:22) and "Let us . . . come boldly unto the throne of grace, that we may obtain mercy, and find grace to help in time of need" (Hebrews 4:16).

Do you know all the blessed meaning of the mercy seat? Our hearts may well throb with loving praise as we think of all this means. "I love the Lord, because he hath heard my voice and my supplications. Because he hath inclined his ear unto me, therefore will I call upon him as long as I live" (Psalm 116:1-2).

The Ark of the Covenant

Let us look at the ark. It is the special type of Christ. He is the sacrifice and the glory and the very center of salvation and of reconciliation with God. The highest meaning of this ancient Tabernacle is the everlasting gospel. So this ark and everything about it was a type of Christ and salvation. The mercy seat was the lid of the ark, and the cherubim were the expansion of the mercy seat. So Jesus Christ is the first and the last, the substance, the Alpha and Omega of that glorious world of which this was the picture.

There was nothing in the Holy of Holies but the ark and its accompaniments. And when we get to heaven we shall see only Jesus. If we look at the Father, we will see Jesus as the fullness of His glory. The angels wait on Him. There is nothing in heaven but Jesus, and there ought to be nothing on earth but Him. We ought to be able to say, "Jesus, fairest among ten thousand, the One altogether lovely. There is none that I desire beside Him." And Jesus fills up all the heart if we will let Him. He is big enough for the altar of sacrifice, big enough for the Holy of Holies, big enough for our little hearts.

Then this glorious ark was the leader of the people. It was the constant pledge of guidance and victory. Wherever Israel went, it went before them. There was a short time when Moses got a little anxious, and he said to his brother-in-law, Hobab, "Leave us not, I pray thee; forasmuch as thou knowest how we are to encamp in the wilderness, and thou mayest be to us instead of eyes" (Numbers 10:31). God said nothing then, but when Israel departed, it was the ark that led them. So Moses saw that the ark was to be the guide, "to search out a resting place for them" (10:33).

Again, when Israel came to Jordan's stormy tide, and swollen waters flowed between them and the promised land, as that ark entered the waters, they were swept aside and Israel went forward in triumph. The ark stands for Jesus, our mighty Leader, the Captain of our salvation.

When we come to the swollen tides of trouble, He will carry us through. When the river overflows its banks in the Jordan of death, it too shall roll asunder, and He shall lead on, the mighty conqueror of death. Jesus declared, "If a man keep my saying, he shall never taste of death" (John 8:52). That person will say: "Where is death? I cannot see it. I cannot see even the traces of the river. There is nothing here but Jesus. There is nothing here but the gates of heaven. Death is all gone!"

And, yet again, that ark contained God's perfect righteousness. There were three things in the ark: the table of the covenant; the rod of Aaron that budded; and the pot of manna taken from the wilderness as a memorial.

The first of these teaches us that Jesus Christ, our ark, had in His very heart and as His very nature, the perfect righteousness of God. The divine law was enshrined in His bosom and so perfectly kept that He brought in a perfect righteousness. He is the only one who has kept or can keep God's perfect law. You remember that the first tables of law were broken. When God gave the law to Adam, Adam broke it. When He gave the law to Moses, it was kept in the ark. So under the new dispensation, Jesus has come down to keep the law. Though it has been the witness of our sin, yet He has fulfilled it.

This is an old story, but it will be told as long as mankind lives, and it will ever be new to some. So I tell it again now. The only way anyone can be saved is by obtaining Christ's righteousness. This is justification.

But there is another thought greater than this. It is not enough for Jesus Christ to keep the law for you, but Jesus Christ wants to come into your heart and keep the law *in* you. And so, not only was the law in the ark, but the ark was in the sanctuary. If you are the dwelling place of the Holy Spirit, in the very center of your soul Jesus is enshrined, just as the ark was in the heart of the Tabernacle. But in the very heart of the ark the law was enshrined; and so the very holiness of Jesus will be enshrined in you if He is in you.

Open your heart and let Christ come in and bring with Him His righteousness and holiness. If Christ is in you, His holiness is in you, and He keeps everything. This is the secret of divine holiness—Christ in the heart, our life and righteousness.

There was another thing in the ark: the rod that budded. This was the picture of Aaron's priesthood, and the buds represented its freshness. It was always new. It represents Jesus at God's right hand praying for us. And the buds on the rod suggest the freshness of Christ's intercessions.

Every morning there is something new. In your heart today there are roses that never bloomed before, there are lilies whose sweet fragrance never breathed until today. There are little dewdrops just come to refresh your soul! Here are the fresh blossoms of peace and joy and healing. "In the beauties of holiness from the womb of the morning: thou hast the dew of thy youth" (Psalm 110:3). Have you been breathing these flowers? Then there is nothing unclean in your heart. Have you been bathing in these dewdrops? Then everything is fresh with you today.

The pot of manna means His constant provision—heavenly bread ever kept for you. There may be no bread on your table, but there is bread inside.

It was very remarkable that when this ark was taken to the temple of Solomon, two of the things were taken out and only one remained. In the wilderness it had the three, but when it was removed to the top of Mount Moriah, the pot of manna and the rod were taken out, and nothing was left but the law. When we get home, we shall not want any more manna, nor shall we have the buds. They will all have become the glorious fruits of paradise. Instead of the dewdrops and the flowers and the promises of fruit, we shall have the tree that yields her fruit every month.

The Cherubim

Again, there were the cherubim that over-shadowed the mercy seat with their four faces—the lion, the ox, the man and the eagle. They represented the human-heartedness of the man, the strength of the ox, the majesty of the lion and the flight of the eagle. They are attributes of Jesus Christ, but they also belong to His brethren. They are the picture of the glory of the redeemed to which we are marching on. By and by we will be as kingly as Jesus, we will be as strong as Jesus, we will be as lofty as Jesus, we will be as spotless as the Son of Man. God put the picture there that we might see it, might be reminded of it, might keep our eye on it. He put it there that it might keep us from everything low and mean. He put it there that we might know our destiny.

Finally, through the wings of these glorious cherubim shone the light of the Skekinah, the presence of God Himself. That is the best of all. That is the light which shall no more go down. That is the sun which shall no more withdraw its shining. God shall be our everlasting light. By and by that light shall be brighter than ten thousand suns, and even in its reflected glory, the righteous ones shall shine forth as the sun in the kingdom of their Father.

Live in the inner Holy of Holies. The door is open all the time. Let your earthly life be in heaven and in the fullness of heaven's grace and glory. Keep your hopes high; there is something better yet. Keep your eye upon the goal, for where your treasure is, there will your heart be also.